MW00744611

DAILY BREAD FOR GIRLS AND BOYS

Living for God

Art by Sam Butcher

Copyright © 1997
Child Evangelism Fellowship® Inc.

Contents

Every Day I Want to Show I Love Jesus

Hide and Seek Words ☐

As you read your Bible try to find these hidden words:

"Believe on the Lord Jesus Christ"

Who Can Follow Jesus?

"If you want to be a follower of the Lord Jesus, first you must believe on Him," Lisa's Sunday school teacher said.

Lisa thought, *Why of course I believe on Jesus; I know He used to live on earth.*

But then the teacher continued, "The kind of believing I'm talking about is to believe He is God's Son. You need to believe that He died on the cross to take the punishment for *your* sins so you can become one of God's children. You must believe that He rose again and is now in Heaven with His Father. If you believe this you will become part of God's family. His Holy Spirit will live in your heart. You will love the Lord Jesus and want to please Him."

Do you believe God's Son died for you? Tell Him. Then you can become His follower today!

Hide and Seek Words ☐

As you read your Bible try to find these hidden words:

"Jesus . . . saith . . . Follow me"

God's Love Magnet

Have you ever played with a magnet? It's fun, isn't it? Things jump right up to meet the magnet, and then hang on.

Sometimes Jesus said to His disciples, "Follow me." Other times He just looked at them and they followed—like steel drawn to a magnet! His *love* is the magnet for no one loves us like the Lord Jesus. That "love magnet" is still drawing people close to Him.

"But Mother," Cindy puzzled, "how can we follow Jesus now? We can't even see Him."

"No, we can't," Mother answered, "but we

follow Him by letting Him guide us through knowing His Word, the Bible."

The Lord Jesus is saying to you, "Follow Me." Are you following?

Hide and Seek Words ☐

As you read your Bible try to find these hidden words:

"...the holy Scriptures...are able to make thee wise"

Read the Directions

"Oh, Matt," Marcie exclaimed to her twin, "isn't it exciting to be in a Christmas play? I'm kind of scared, too, though. I'm afraid I'll mess it up."

"I don't know why you should. All you have to do is follow the directions. See; here are mine. I'm the third shepherd so I follow Tracy. It tells me what side I come in on, what I do, and even what I'm supposed to wear. See; nothing to it, if you follow the directions!"

God has given directions to those who follow Him. You don't have to be afraid that you won't know what to do in life. His directions are in the Bible, but you must read them! They're never too hard to follow.

Hide and Seek Words ☐
As you read your Bible try to find these hidden words:
"Be . . . followers [imitators] of God"

To Follow Is to Imitate

With a book in his hand, three-year-old Sammy pushed a stool up to the easy chair. Seating himself, he wiggled forward until he could prop his feet up on the stool. Now, almost lying on the chair, he opened his book (upside down) and pretended to read.

Father found Sammy like this a few minutes later and he smiled to himself. He knew what Sammy was doing; he was imitating him. That is exactly the way his father liked to relax after coming home from work!

Do you imitate your father? Do you imitate your Heavenly Father? He wants you to be full of love and kindness as He is. Your Heavenly Father will never do anything wrong, so you can imitate Him in *everything*.

Hide and Seek Words ☐

As you read your Bible try to find these hidden words:

"... ye should follow his steps"

What Would Jesus Do?

"Must I read my Bible EVERY day?" pouted Jamie. "I just don't *feel like it.*"

"No," Mother said thoughtfully, "you don't *have* to read your Bible if you really don't want to. For you won't hear God's voice too well when you feel that way. But, what was it you were asking me just a few minutes ago?"

"You mean about our Bible verse for Sunday school this week?"

"Yes," answered Mother. "Didn't you say you wanted to be like the Lord Jesus and follow His steps?" Jamie nodded his head up and down.

"Do you think there would ever be a day the Lord Jesus would not want to hear from His Heavenly Father?"

Jamie didn't even stop to answer! He quickly picked up the Bible, took it to his room, and began reading. He *did* want to know what God wanted to say to him *every day!*

Do you wonder how to follow in Jesus' steps?

It will always help you to be good and true
If you ask yourself, what would Jesus do?

Hide and Seek Words ☐

As you read your Bible try to find these hidden words:

"Ye ought . . . to please God"

Because He Wants Us to

Many years ago in China a missionary was awakened by a loud knocking at his door. Knowing that men were afraid to walk about after dark, he was surprised to find two young boys standing there.

"Why have you come?" he asked.

"Our teacher is sick and we've come for some medicine."

"But why didn't some men come?" the missionary asked.

"They were afraid," the boys answered.

"And aren't you afraid?"

"We are; but we came because Jesus would want us to do this."

Love for the Lord Jesus will make us want to please Him—even if we are afraid, or if others think we're foolish. Pleasing Jesus comes first!

Hide and Seek Words ☐

As you read your Bible try to find these hidden words:

"If we confess . . . he is faithful . . . to forgive"

I'm Sorry

"Why, Jill, whatever is the matter?" Carol asked her little sister.

"I feel awful! Jesus will *never* forgive me," sobbed Jill. "I was so terrible in church today. I laughed and whispered, even while Pastor Brown was praying. And Mrs. Bailey was there for the first time, but I heard her say . . . " (now Jill cried harder than ever) "I . . . I heard her say she was *never* coming back, because some girl made too much noise. And I'm the one!"

"That *was* terrible," Carol agreed, "but the Lord Jesus has promised to forgive you if you're sorry."

Sometimes, even His followers do things which are wrong. But when you do, you need to talk to Him in prayer and ask Him to forgive you. He has promised that He will!

Hide and Seek Words ☐

As you read your Bible try to find these hidden words:

"Continue in prayer"

Talk and Listen

"Hey, Mom, look!" Richy shouted. He had just arrived home from a parade honoring one of his baseball heroes. "Jackie signed my baseball mitt. And I got to *talk* to him, too! Oh, man; what a thrill!"

Yes, it IS thrilling to talk to someone we love and look up to, especially a great leader.

Jesus is our Leader. It's wonderful to talk to Him in prayer! He doesn't speak to us out loud, but He speaks to us through His Word and His Holy Spirit. His Spirit brings God's thoughts to our minds. He gives us that beautiful feeling of God's love, deep down inside. The more we talk to Him the closer He is to us.

Talk to God many times every day. He hears even the softest whispers, and knows the "thought prayers" in your mind!

Hide and Seek Words ☐

As you read your Bible try to find these hidden words:

" ...thou art with me"

You Can Trust Him!

Happy, the fluffy white lamb, wasn't feeling like his name. He had just reached under a bush to get a mouth full of green grass and when he tried to pull back, the thorny branches held him fast. Happy wiggled this way and that but with each wiggle he was caught more securely.

"Baa! baa!" His cries became more terrified all the time.

Then he felt a hand holding him and the kind voice of the shepherd said, "Happy, don't be afraid. I'll get you loose."

It was only a few minutes until he was free again and "baaing" his thank you.

The Lord Jesus is our Good Shepherd—our Leader. If you get into a frightening spot, call upon Him. He has promised to help you.

Hide and Seek Words ☐

As you read your Bible try to find these hidden words:

" . . . angels . . . to keep [guard] thee"

God's Helpers

The king was troubled. He loved and respected Daniel. But he had been tricked into making a law which sent Daniel into a lions' den! All night the king worried. Would Daniel's God be able to protect him from those hungry lions?

At the first light of day the king hurried to the den and called, "Oh, Daniel, did your God deliver you?" And the voice came back, "My God hath sent his angel, and hath shut the lions'

mouths." (Read Daniel's story in Daniel 6:16-23.)

Yes, the angels are God's helpers. Like Daniel, we too have been given guardian angels to watch over us. This is another proof of God's love for those who follow Him.

Hide and Seek Words ☐

As you read your Bible try to find these hidden words:

"...where I am, there ye may be also"

A Beautiful Home

"I wish you weren't leaving, Daddy," Scott said sadly.

"Let's try not to think about the leaving part. Just think of that nice home I'm getting ready for you and Mother and Jill. Remember, I've promised to fix one of the basement rooms for your own special workshop. Then when everything is ready, I'll come back to move all of you there."

Jesus' followers were sorry to hear that He was going to leave them to go back to Heaven. But Jesus said, "In my Father's house are many mansions;...I go to prepare a place for you...I will come again, and receive you unto myself, that where I am, there ye may be also" (John 14:2, 3).

Isn't that happy news? And it's for *all* His followers.

Follow the Lord Jesus closely so that you will not be ashamed when He comes!

Hide and Seek Words ☐

As you read your Bible try to find these hidden words:

"Not slothful [lazy]"

My Father Works

What a busy place it is in the underground home of the ants. Ants are scurrying here and there—each with its own job to do. Some care for the queen, the eggs, and the baby ants. Some stand guard, while others are out hunting food. Many are building new tunnels and rooms to enlarge their home. Yes, they all, from the youngest to the oldest, work at the tasks they can do best. This must have been the reason why King Solomon told lazy people to study the ants and learn from them!

Jesus believed in working. He said, "My Father works and I work" (John 5:17). As His followers we will work, too.

Our hands to work for Jesus,

Our feet to take us there,

Our mouth to tell Him "thank You"—

For strength to do our share.

Hide and Seek Words ☐

As you read your Bible try to find these hidden words:

". . . let us . . . love . . . in deed"

The Way to Prove It

"I love you, Mommy," Elizabeth said. Mother was lying down with a bad headache, while little brother played in the corner of the room. Elizabeth ran outside to play, slamming the door behind her.

Five minutes later Elizabeth's twin sister, Emily, came into her mother's room. "I love you, Mommy. Here, let me put a cool cloth on your head. I'll take little brother outdoors so you can rest better."

Now, who do you think really loved her mother the most?

The Lord Jesus proved His love by the deeds He did here on earth. People came to Him with their problems, knowing that He cared. Even the children could feel His love and were not afraid.

Let us love like Jesus loved—not just with words, but by our deeds (the things we do).

Hide and Seek Words ☐

As you read your Bible try to find these hidden words:

"Do good . . . and your reward shall be great"

Extra Rewards

Carol's eyes were shining as she opened the door for her mother who had just arrived back from shopping. She couldn't wait to see if Mother noticed all the work she had done while she was gone.

And sure enough, she did. "Why, Carol," Mother exclaimed, "you cleaned the house for me; everything looks so nice! And you washed the dishes, too. Thank you very much, my dear."

"I made you a cake too, Mommy," Carol said.

"Wonderful! I think for a reward, we'll go out for hamburgers and french fries. Then I'll buy some ice cream to have with your cake."

"I didn't do it for a reward, Mommy; I did it because I love you," Carol said. But she got a reward, too.

We do things for the Lord Jesus because we love Him. And He has promised to reward us besides!

Hide and Seek Words ☐

As you read your Bible try to find these hidden words:

"Be thou [you be] an example"

An Example

Brian saw his little brother, Mark, and two of his friends looking over a fence by a broken-down house. Wondering what the three boys were up to, he listened behind a bush.

"Aw, come on, Mark; don't be chicken," one of the boys said. "It would be fun to see what this old house looks like inside. No one is around to see us."

"But the signs say KEEP OUT, and my big brother says only foolish people disobey signs. Anyway, someone *will* see us; God will." Mark turned to leave, and even though they were still grumbling, the other two followed.

Brian felt like clapping his hands. *Good for Mark,* he said to himself. *He was sure one of God's examples.*

Does your ex-
ample help oth-
ers do what is
right?

Hide and Seek Words ☐

As you read your Bible try to find these hidden words:

"Let us go into the house of the Lord"

The Special Day

"Hi, John! Hi, Mrs. Tanner!" John's friend Tim greeted them. "We're spending a day at the state fair and Mom said John could come, too."

"She did! Great!" John exclaimed. "What day are you going?"

"Sunday," Tim answered.

"Sunday?" And John stopped smiling.

"John can go if he wishes," Mrs. Tanner said. She wasn't a Christian so she didn't care where John spent Sunday.

But John had a struggle going on inside. He loved the Lord Jesus and knew his place was in church on Sunday. John also knew there would be great fun at the fair. Finally he made up his mind. "Thank you for asking me, Tim, but I'm God's child and Sunday is the special day we set apart to worship in His house."

Was that the right answer? How do you know?

Hide and Seek Words ☐

As you read your Bible try to find these hidden words:

" . . . **reverence [show honor to] my sanctuary**"

A Place Set Apart

When the Lord Jesus was on earth He went into the temple of God and saw something which made Him very unhappy. Men were buying and selling in the temple, and were even doing it dishonestly. The Bible tells us that Jesus made a scourge (a whip) of small cords and made the men leave the temple. He told them His Father's house was to be a house of prayer but they had made it a den of thieves!

The church is a place set apart to worship (love and praise) our Savior. One of the ways you can show your love to Him is by your reverence or respect for His house. Remember, even though you cannot see the Lord Jesus, He sees what is happening when you are in God's house. What are you making your church to be? Are you behaving in church in a way that would please the Lord Jesus?

Hide and Seek Words ☐

As you read your Bible try to find these hidden words:

" . . .obey your parents"

Especially for You

Jesus gave some rules especially for children. One was "Obey your parents." There are many ways to obey, but only one right way!

Many of the boys and girls from Midland grade school were told to come straight home from school. Let's listen to some of the different ways they had of obeying.

Greg said, "Guess I'd better get home or I won't get to watch television for a week."

Melody said, "I want a new dress, so I'd better get right home to keep on the good side of Mom."

Joel grumbled, "Guess I'd better go home but I sure wish I could stay and play. My folks never let me do anything I want to."

Karen said, "Mamma told me to come straight home, so I'll see you tomorrow." With a smile and a wave she hurried on her way.

Karen not only obeyed by her *actions* but with her *heart*. That is the right way!

Hide and Seek Words ☐

As you read your Bible try to find these hidden words:

"Let the words of my mouth . . . be acceptable"

The Troublesome Door

There is a door that each of us seems to have trouble with. It swings open at the wrong time, and . . . what comes through that door! Sometimes it hurts others, and often it may hurt you. Sometimes it starts fights! Other times it makes someone cry. It may make your parents and teachers shake their heads sadly. The Bible says it is like a poison and sometimes like a fire out of control. This door is your *mouth*.

David asked God to put a watch or a guard by his *mouth-door*. He wanted his words to please God.

Today in your Quiet Time with God, ask the Lord Jesus to put a guard at your *mouth-door* so that you will speak only what is right and good.

Hide and Seek Words ☐

As you read your Bible try to find these hidden words:

" . . . **putting away lying**"

The Truth

All the evidence pointed to Jeremy. He had been the only one in the room between noon and four o'clock when the old half-dollar belonging to his grandfather's collection had disappeared. Still, no one was surprised when they discovered the real thief was not Jeremy but their pet blue jay!

You see, Jeremy was in the habit of trying to be like his Heavenly Father. So when he had quietly said, "No, I didn't take the half-dollar," they knew he hadn't. They knew that the truth of the Lord Jesus was in him.

Our Heavenly Father speaks the truth,

I'll trust His Word each day.

I wonder if those who hear my voice

Can believe each word I say.

Hide and Seek Words ☐

As you read your Bible try to find these hidden words:

"A merry heart doeth good"

The Secret of Happiness

A little boy said to his mother, "I couldn't make sister happy 'cause I couldn't fix her doll. But I made myself happy trying to make her happy."

Another boy, speaking of his handicapped brother, said, "I make Jim happy. He laughs and that makes me happy. Then I laugh!"

Following Jesus helps us make a big circle of happiness. First, Jesus gives us happiness. We show our happiness by trying to make others happy. Then we become happier still!

The more you give, the more you get—

A secret just for you;

For as you share some joy with others,

You'll have a lot more, too.

Hide and Seek Words ☐

As you read your Bible try to find these hidden words:

"God loveth a cheerful giver"

Giving Back

"Pastor," Lance frowned impatiently, "Why aren't the lights turned on?"

"Since we didn't have enough money to pay the electric bill the company turned the electricity off. It seems some people have been stealing from God!"

"Stealing from God?" Lance exclaimed.

"Yes, they're keeping their offering money that belongs to God and spending it for themselves."

Lance was thinking of some offering he had spent on ice cream and the dollar he should have given to God out of the ten he had earned. "I'll never do it again—never do it again—never—"

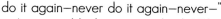

Lance suddenly sat up in bed. "Oh, only a dream," he sighed with relief. But he got the message! He would gladly give the money to God that belonged to Him from now on.

Are *you* a cheerful giver?

Hide and Seek Words ☐

As you read your Bible try to find these hidden words:

"Neglect not [don't ignore] the gift that is in thee"

Gifts for Him

"1-2-3-4, 1-2-3-4," Scott counted as he practiced his piano lesson. Then he missed a note and banged both hands down on the keys.

"Mom," he called, "do I *have* to practice?"

"Yes, you do," she answered. "Perhaps it wouldn't seem so hard, though, if you remembered you were doing it for Jesus' sake."

Mother continued, "You see, God has given each of us a special gift. For some it might be the ability to speak well, or the ability to understand mathematics or science, but to you He gave a musical ability. As His follower He wants you to study and perfect this gift so you can use it for Him!"

Ask God to show you what special gift He's given you and to help you work on it for Him.

Hide and Seek Words ☐

As you read your Bible try to find these hidden words:

"Giving thanks always"

Thank You

The switchboard operator had been trying to reach a certain number all afternoon. She was so tired of hearing the lady say, "Will you please try the number again?" Finally she was able to get the call through.

After a few minutes the switchboard light went on. It was the same lady who had been calling and calling and calling. *Oh, no!* the operator thought to herself. But her frown quickly changed to a smile. The voice on the other end of the line said, "I just want to thank you for being so patient and taking so much trouble to get my number."

The operator was so surprised that she could only mumble, "Er-a-yes, ma'am."

How many times do you give the Lord Jesus and others the happy surprise of saying "thank you"? Today in your Quiet Time with God, remember to tell the Lord Jesus "thank you" for being such a wonderful Savior.

Hide and Seek Words ☐

As you read your Bible try to find these hidden words:

" . . . **be ye kind**"

Pass It On

Jim is a bird watcher. Once he became very interested in a flock of chewinks (sometimes called finches). One of the chewinks acted strangely. Jim noticed that even though this bird was bigger than the rest, he did not pick up food for himself. He was fed by the rest of the birds!

After Jim had watched for several days, his curiosity got the best of him and he caught the bird. What a surprise awaited Jim. The bird wasn't lazy. He had a bill that was crossed at the end. If the other birds had not fed him, he would have starved to death!

Ask the Lord Jesus to put kindness in your heart so that you will never be too busy to help someone in need.

Dear Jesus, You've been so kind to me.

Help me pass it on.

That I can be much more like Thee.

Help me pass it on.

Hide and Seek Words ☐
As you read your Bible try to find these hidden words:

"There is no respect of persons [no favorites] with God"

No Favorites

"Before we take a final vote, let's have a discussion."

The Capital Hill Boys' Club was trying to decide if they would ask the boy who had just moved into the neighborhood to join their club.

"He seems like a nice kid," Stephen commented.

"His clothes are so different," someone jeered.

"Yes, but they're clean," answered Stephen.

"He talks funny; you can hardly understand him."

"We could help him learn our language."

And so the discussion went on, some laughing at the boy's odd looks, ways and speech differences which Stephen was ready to overlook. He knew the Lord Jesus would not have him judge the new boy by his looks, speech or race.

God has no favorites. He loves everyone the same. So of course, that is the best way for us, too.

Hide and Seek Words ☐

As you read your Bible try to find these hidden words:

"Recompense [pay back] to no man evil"

The Right Way to "Pay Back"

At the sound of footsteps, Sarah quickly closed her bag of candy and hid it under the sofa pillow. "If that's Jared, he's not going to get any, since he's too selfish to let me ride his bike."

Just then the telephone rang and Sarah heard her mother say, "Surely, Mrs. Green, I'd be glad to look after Andy for you for awhile."

"Mother!" Sarah exclaimed after her mother had hung up, "you're going to help her after what she did to you?"

"Yes, dear. It's not Jesus' way to pay back evil for evil, but rather to love and do good to those that do wrong to us. That is what He did. He even died for those that hated Him!"

Sarah was quiet for a few minutes. When Jared came, guess what she said to him.

Hide and Seek Words ☐

As you read your Bible try to find these hidden words:

" . . . they have not heard"

Don't Keep It a Secret

We usually think that Jesus' followers were brave men and women who were afraid of nothing. But that wasn't always true! Nicodemus first came to Jesus at night—perhaps because he was afraid. A man named Joseph loved Jesus and followed Him, but he did it in such a way that those who hated Jesus wouldn't know about it. Finally, though, both men showed their love for Jesus by taking His body from the cross. Tenderly they cared for it and laid it in Joseph's own tomb.

It's better to be a secret follower of Jesus than not to be a follower at all. But it is *best* to let everyone know! How shall they believe if they have not heard?

Hide and Seek Words ☐

As you read your Bible try to find these hidden words:

"Go . . . to thy friends, and tell them"

Go and Tell

"Oh, Angie", Rebecca beamed, "do you know what *my* daddy did for me over the weekend? He fixed a corner of the garage for my very own playhouse. Then he made some wooden boxes into a cupboard and table and chairs, and let me paint them—all by myself! He's the nicest daddy ever!"

Yes, it's good to have a "nicest" father. Those who follow Jesus and belong to the family of God know what a wonderful Heavenly Father they have, too. But others do not know, so we must tell them.

Tell others what God has done for *you*, a special prayer He answered, a time He helped you remember during a hard test, or a time you were afraid but He took all your fear away. Tell them so they will want to believe on the Lord Jesus and become part of God's family, too!

Hide and Seek Words ☐

As you read your Bible try to find these hidden words:

" . . . endure hardness, as a good soldier"

Never Give Up!

Many years ago a ship was in trouble, with only one way left to signal help. A message was sealed in a tiny tube and fastened to the leg of a little pigeon. Away it flew toward home.

But things changed for the worse! Soon the pigeon flew into a storm which blew it off course. It seemed as if the pigeon would have to give up. But no! Tired, battered and bruised, it finally arrived home. The message was read and help was rushed to the ship in trouble.

It is not easy to be a soldier of the Lord Jesus. Satan will try to make you quit by sending storms of fear and doubt. He will try to make you think his way is easier. But being Jesus' soldier brings the greatest joy here on earth *and* happiness in Heaven when you leave this life.

Lord, Help Me Love Others
As Much As I Love Myself

Hide and Seek Words ☐

As you read your Bible try to find these hidden words:

"God is love"

God Loves You

"Keith! Where are you?" called Doug.

"On the hill," answered Keith.

Doug raced up to where his friend was sitting. "Why do you always come here?" he panted as he dropped down in the grass.

"You know why," answered Keith softly.

"Yes, guess I do," said Doug. "Your parents fighting again?"

Keith nodded. Tears glistened in his eyes.

"I'm sorry, Keith," said Doug quietly. "But no matter what happens, remember God loves you."

Keith replied angrily, "No, He doesn't! Nobody loves me."

"Yes, God does!" insisted Doug. "The Bible is God's Word and it says He loves you more than you can ever know."

Keith looked up through the leaves of the trees into the bright blue of the sky. "I wish I could believe that," he whispered.

Hide and Seek Words ☐

As you read your Bible try to find these hidden words:

"...love is of God"

Where Is Love?

"God does love you, Keith," assured Doug. "Love comes from God and without God there is no love."

Keith looked thoughtful. "Maybe that's why my mom and dad don't love me," he reasoned. "They don't believe in God and they sure don't like each other."

Doug said, "They don't know God loves them."

"Maybe you're right," said Keith slowly. "I don't think they really mean to be so hateful. It's just that they are so unhappy and so lonely they can't help but be awful to each other and to me. Maybe if they knew about the love that comes from God...maybe if they could get some of that love for themselves..." Keith's eyes began to shine. "Maybe...just maybe...things could really be great!"

Hide and Seek Words ☐
As you read your Bible try to find these hidden words:

" . . . he first loved us"

Love Him Back!

"Doug," asked Keith carefully, "how can I know God really loves me and my parents?"

Quickly Doug replied, "You can know He does because He says so in His Word."

"How can I get some of God's love to my parents?" asked Keith anxiously.

"You can begin by believing God loves you and by loving Him back," Doug explained. "He loved you first; now you can return His love by believing what He says. Then you can tell your parents about Him."

"I don't know anything about God," admitted Keith. "I want to love God, but you'll have to tell me about Him. God's just got to help me and my mom and dad!"

"He will," promised Doug. "He loves you and He wants you to love Him."

Hide and Seek Words ☐
As you read your Bible try to find these hidden words:

"God so loved . . . he gave his only . . . Son"

God Came to Earth

"God is the strongest, most powerful person there is. He has control over everything," said Doug. "He can make anything or anybody do whatever He wants. But God is also love. He wanted someone He could love. That's why He made people. He wanted to show His love to them.

"God lets people have the choice of loving and obeying Him or hating and disobeying Him. God's Son, Jesus Christ, came to earth Himself as a person. The Lord Jesus explained God's love to men. He let men who hated Him kill Him so that He could take our punishment for sin.

Three days after He died He came back to life. Then He went to Heaven to get it ready for the people who love Him."

Hide and Seek Words □

As you read your Bible try to find these hidden words:

"... while we were yet sinners, Christ died for us"

Jesus Died for You

"Keith," Doug explained, "the Lord Jesus died in *your* place for *your* sin."

Keith looked puzzled and asked, "What's sin?"

Doug answered, "Sin is anything we do that is wrong, no matter how small it is. Our sin separates us from God."

Keith was upset. "But everybody does things wrong!"

Doug agreed, "Yes, they do, and anyone who sins should die for it. But Jesus has never sinned. Because of God's great love, He let His Son die in our place. All we need to do is believe that He did this. When we ask the Lord Jesus to take our sin away, He does. God sees us just as if we had never done anything wrong. Then we belong to God."

Keith repeated, "I have to believe that Jesus died in my place for my sin. Then will I belong to God?"

"Right," Doug nodded.

Hide and Seek Words ☐

As you read your Bible try to find these hidden words:

"As far as the east is from the west"

God Does It Right

"God hates sin," explained Doug, "and anyone who has sinned is separated from God. The Lord Jesus takes our sin away when we ask Him to. Then God can accept us as if we had never done anything wrong."

"What does Jesus do with our sin?" asked Keith.

Doug answered, "God's Word, the Bible, says that He takes it as far away as the east is from the west. And that's about as far away as anything can get."

Keith laughed, "I guess when God does a job, He does it real good."

Doug agreed, "He sure does, Keith, and the job He wants to do right now is to let you know He loves you. He wants you to ask Jesus to take your sin away. Then *you* can become a child of God and start loving Him back."

Hide and Seek Words ☐
As you read your Bible try to find these hidden words:

" . . . what manner of love . . . that we should be called the sons of God"

The Greatest Thing!

"I really want Jesus to take my sin away," said Keith with deep feeling. "How can I ask Him?"

"Any way you want; just tell Him," replied Doug.

Keith stood to his feet and looked up into the sky as far as he could see. "Lord Jesus," he prayed, "please take my sin away so God can accept me and I can belong to You. I want to love You back because You love me and I want to belong to God. . . . I guess that's all."

Keith dropped back down on the grass. "It worked, Doug. I know it did. Something happened inside of me! I'm one of God's children now." Keith shouted, "It's the greatest thing that's ever happened to me!"

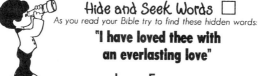

Hide and Seek Words ☐
As you read your Bible try to find these hidden words:

"I have loved thee with an everlasting love"

Love Forever

"I feel so good!" sighed Keith as he lay on the soft grass. Slowly he put his hands behind his head. "I wonder how long it will last."

Doug was surprised. "What do you mean, 'how long it will last'?"

Keith rolled over and looked at Doug. "Whenever something good happens to me, it always has to stop. This is the best thing of all and I'm afraid it will stop too."

Doug assured him, "Keith, you have just become a child of God and God has promised to love you forever. God never changes. If He says He will love you forever, that means always and always. His love will never stop."

Keith said thoughtfully, "God will love me from right now until always. This good thing will never end!"

Hide and Seek Words ☐

As you read your Bible try to find these hidden words:

"There is no fear in love"

Don't Be Afraid

A frown came over Keith's face. "What if I do something wrong again, would God stop letting me be His child?"

Doug answered, "No! I guess it's kind of like when you disobey your parents at home. You're still their child no matter what. But to make things right, you need to tell them you're sorry. The same thing is true with God. You need to tell Him you're sorry (1 John 1:9). He will forgive you and help you not to do it again. Don't be afraid, God won't stop loving you. You're His child from now on."

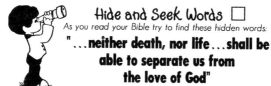

Hide and Seek Words ☐

As you read your Bible try to find these hidden words:

"...neither death, nor life...shall be able to separate us from the love of God"

It's Ours for Keeps!

"Keith," explained Doug, "there is a verse in God's Word that says nothing can separate us from God's love. All the time we're alive, His love is with us. When we die, His love is there. Angels can't keep God's love from us. Satan and all his helpers can't. We ourselves can't stop God's love for us. In fact, no matter what happens to us or where we are, God's love is with us. It doesn't matter how high in the sky or how deep in the ocean we are, His love still reaches us. God's love is the greatest power in the world, and it's all ours!"

"Whew!" whistled Keith. "That's about the surest thing there is. Nobody else can make a promise like that."

"That's right," said Doug. "Only God can and that's why I want to love Him and obey Him!"

Hide and Seek Words ☐

As you read your Bible try to find these hidden words:

"God hath prepared for them that love him"

You Can't Imagine It!

Doug remembered, "There's another verse in God's Word that says God has wonderful things planned for us because we love Him. It says that we have never seen or heard or understood the things that God is getting ready for them that love Him."

Keith was excited. "That sounds great, doesn't it? I wonder when and where all of this will happen."

Doug reasoned, "Probably in Heaven, but God helps us here on earth too. Maybe it's both here and in Heaven."

Keith wondered, "What will Heaven be like?"

Doug replied, "I don't know, except the best thing of all will be that we can see and talk to the Lord Jesus. Maybe that's what God means. We can't possibly know how great it will be to see the Lord Jesus all the time!"

Hide and Seek Words ☐
As you read your Bible try to find these hidden words:

"Love . . . **God with all thy heart**"

Love Him Most of All

"God has given us His love and a way to become His children; He has promised us so much. What can we do to please Him?" asked Keith.

Doug said thoughtfully, "God wants to be first in our lives. I guess He wants us to love Him more than anything or anyone else in the world."

Keith was astonished. "How can we do that?"

Doug answered, "We can't. God the Holy Spirit came to live in you and me when we became God's children. He will help us
obey. He will help us
love God more than
anything else. We can't
do it ourselves, but with
the help of the Holy
Spirit, we can put God
first in everything!"

Hide and Seek Words ☐

As you read your Bible try to find these hidden words:

"Love him with all thy . . . strength"

Learn to Know and Obey

Keith said anxiously, "I want to show God I love Him, but how can I know what I should do?"

Doug answered, "You should read His Word, the Bible."

Keith was excited. "Hey, I've got a Bible at home. I'm going to go get it and read it!"

Doug grinned. "Good! Plan to read part of it every day so you can learn what God wants you to do. It will be hard to keep doing it because Satan doesn't want you to please God. Satan is God's enemy. He doesn't want anyone to show love to God. But the Holy Spirit will help you learn what God wants you to do. He will give you strength to obey God's Word."

Hide and Seek Words ☐
As you read your Bible try to find these hidden words:

"...this is love...walk after his commandments"

Want to Obey

Keith reasoned, "We show God we love Him by learning about Him—we learn what He wants us to do. Then we do it."

Doug agreed. "It sounds simple enough, but it's impossible to do."

Keith added, "That's where the Holy Spirit comes in."

"Hey!" exclaimed Doug, "You're really catching on. The Holy Spirit gives us the power to obey God's orders. But we have to *want* to obey them."

Keith summed it up. "We have to make the choice of obeying God, then the Holy Spirit gives us the power to do it. Whew! I sure hope all this works."

Doug assured him, "It does!"

"Well," said Keith as he stood up, "the first thing I have to do is find out what God wants me to do."

Hide and Seek Words ☐

As you read your Bible try to find these hidden words:

" . . . love one another;
as I have loved you"

Love Each Other

"Lord Jesus," Keith prayed, "I want to know what I can do to please You. So I'm going to read your Word, the Bible. Help me obey the orders I find from You." Keith started to read, "Love one another as I have loved you." Keith thought, *That's my first order from God. I'm supposed to love other people, like my parents, because God loves me. I must love them no matter what they've done to me.* Keith was upset, "God, I can't do that! You don't know how awful my parents have been to me!" He paused. "But You do know, don't You, Lord Jesus? That's why I saw that order first." Keith bowed his head. "You'll have to help me, Lord Jesus. I can't do it by myself."

Hide and Seek Words ☐

As you read your Bible try to find these hidden words:

"...**he is a liar**"

You Can't Hate Man and Love God

Keith was deeply troubled. "Lord Jesus, I hate my parents. I guess it's because I know they hate me. They just put up with me because they have to. I didn't ask to be born into this world...but...I guess You know all about that. You wanted me to be born, didn't You? You want me to stop hating and start loving my parents. You said in the Bible that I can't hate anyone and love You at the same time, even if I have reasons to hate. If I say I love You and hate someone else, Your Word says I'm a liar."

Keith prayed, "Lord God, help me to stop hating my parents and start loving them...I believe You can do it!"

Hide and Seek Words ☐

As you read your Bible try to find these hidden words:

"Thou shalt love thy neighbor as thyself"

Love Them as You Love Yourself

I can't hate my parents, thought Keith. *Maybe God just means for me to like them a little.* Keith started looking through his Bible for an order from God telling him how much he should care about his parents. He started to read the verses listed under the word *love* in the back of his Bible. At last he found it. "Thou shalt love thy neighbor *as thyself.*" Keith reasoned, "That means I'm supposed to love my neighbor as much as I love myself. So it must mean I'm supposed to love my parents as much as I love myself. I guess I love me better than anyone else. Wow, that's a tall order, Lord Jesus. I can't do it. But I want to. Help me, Lord God, to love my parents as much as I love myself."

Hide and Seek Words ☐

As you read your Bible try to find these hidden words:

"Love worketh no ill"

Love Doesn't Want to Hurt

Keith looked at another verse in his Bible listed under the word *love.* "Love worketh no ill to his neighbor." Keith thought to himself, *Love worketh no ill. That means it doesn't want to hurt or do wrong.* Keith said out loud, "Now I understand why *love* is so opposite from *hate.* When someone hates you they want to hurt you any way they can. Love means that you don't want to hurt someone. You wouldn't do anything that would harm them or make them feel bad."

Keith looked out his bedroom window and prayed, "I'm starting to understand how You want me to feel toward my parents, Lord Jesus.

You don't want me to say or do anything to them that would make them feel bad. I can do that if You help me!"

Hide and Seek Words □

As you read your Bible try to find these hidden words:

"...charity [love] shall cover the multitude of sins"

Love Helps Us to Forgive

Keith found another *love* verse in his Bible. It said, love shall cover many sins. Keith was puzzled. "That's hard to understand." He prayed, "Help me to know what it means, Lord Jesus."

Keith studied the verse a long time. At last he said, "I think it means that when you love someone, you can forgive the wrong things they've done to you. That means that if I really loved my parents, I could forgive the mean things they've done to me." Keith bowed his head, "Help me to forgive the bad things that have happened, God. Help me to show my parents I love them." Keith stood up. "I'm going to do something about my prayers. I'm going to try to show my parents I love them!"

Hide and Seek Words ☐

As you read your Bible try to find these hidden words:

**"When my father and my mother
forsake me, then
the Lord will take me up"**

God Will Keep You

"God! Oh, Lord God!" cried Keith as he ran into his room and threw himself on his bed. "They didn't want my love!" His heart pained inside him. He hurt so much he could only take short quick breaths. "Help me, help me, God."

After a very long time he sat up and wiped his eyes. Suddenly, joy flooded Keith's heart. He cried with happiness, "Lord Jesus, they hurt me, but I didn't want to hurt them back. You've taken my hate away. It's gone! I didn't want to hurt them. Thank You, Lord Jesus, thank You!"

Keith's sadness had turned to joy.

Hide and Seek Words ☐

As you read your Bible try to find these hidden words:

"Charity [love] suffereth long"

Love Is Patient

Keith scratched his head. "I've got to learn more about how to show my parents I love them. I wonder if God's Word has anything to say about that. Once again Keith searched for verses about love listed in the back of his Bible. He was surprised to find a whole chapter about how to show love. It was 1 Corinthians, the thirteenth chapter.

"Wow!" he exclaimed. "This is terrific!" He began to read. "Love suffereth long!" *That means it is patient and calm, not all upset and worried.* Keith looked up. "God is sure going to have to help me with this because I'm always upset and worried about something. I never would have guessed that this would be a way to show love. I've got lots to learn."

Hide and Seek Words ☐

As you read your Bible try to find these hidden words:

"Charity [love] . . . is kind"

Love Is Being Kind to Others

Keith read, "Love is kind." He thought, *Kindness means doing things to help others.* He grinned. *I'm going to try it.* He went into the kitchen where his mother was peeling a squash for supper. "Boy, that looks like a lot of work. Can I help?" Keith asked.

His mother looked up surprised. "Yes, it is quite a job," she said, as she put her knife down and washed her hands. "You certainly can help. Would you mind putting the peelings out in the garbage can?"

"Sure thing," said Keith, as he gathered up the peelings in a newspaper.

"Thanks!" called his mother as he banged out the back door.

Keith smiled to himself. "Maybe I can't say I love them in words, but I can *show* it by the way I act."

Hide and Seek Words ☐
As you read your Bible try to find these hidden words:
"Charity [love] . . . envieth not"

Love Is Not Jealous

Keith opened his Bible to find "Love envieth not." He thought, *Love isn't jealous.* It felt as if an arrow had gone right to his heart. He remembered Doug and his parents. What a great time they always had together. How much they really liked each other. He thought, *Doug's parents try to make me feel welcome too. But I always hold back and feel jealous of them because my parents and I don't have the same kind of closeness.*

Keith bowed his head in shame. "Forgive me, God. I thought it was okay because it wasn't

 THINGS I was jealous of. Help me not to feel mean and jealous toward Doug and his parents. Help me to love them, too."

Hide and Seek Words ☐
As you read your Bible try to find these hidden words:
"Charity [love] . . . is not puffed up"

Love Doesn't Brag

"God sure knows all about humans," laughed Keith as he read his next love-order. "Love is not puffed up." *That's easy; it means I shouldn't try to make myself look big or important. A person trying to brag about himself does try to "puff himself up."* Keith looked at himself in his mirror and puffed out his cheeks. *It sure looks silly,* he thought. *That's what God must think we look like when we try to brag.*

Keith became very serious. "That's a problem I have," he confessed. "I guess it's because Mom

and Dad aren't too interested in anything I do, so I try to get their attention by acting important. Maybe now that I know God loves me so much and is so concerned about me, I won't need to get all 'puffed up.' "

Hide and Seek Words ☐

As you read your Bible try to find these hidden words:

"Charity [love] . . . doth not behave itself unseemly"

Love Is Thoughtful Behavior

I'm going to have to use more of what I've learned about love, thought Keith, as he got ready for supper. *I'll start by trying to make this meal more pleasant than usual.*

"Hello, Mom and Dad!" Keith said as he plopped down on his chair. "Everything sure smells good." He sniffed as he reached for the meat. Keith filled his plate and continued his cheerful chatter in spite of the usual glum silence. After they had finished eating he said, "Mom, the squash was delicious. I guess we make a good squash team, don't we? You cut it up and I clean it up." His mom smiled in spite of herself. "You seem happy," she said.

Keith answered, "I am. I've had something great happen to me. I've become a child of God."

Keith excused himself and left the table as his parents looked at each other in surprise.

Hide and Seek Words ☐
As you read your Bible try to find these hidden words:
"Charity [love] . . . seeketh not her own"

Love Is Unselfish

"Keith!" called his mother. "Would you tell your father to clean up that mess he's making in the garage? He's supposed to be fixing the car!" she fussed.

Keith felt terrible. He did not want to hurt his dad. "God, help me make things better."

Keith walked to the garage. "Hi, Pop!" he called. "What are you doing?" There was no answer from under the hood of the car where his father was working. "I came out to clean up. Where do you want me to start?"

Slowly his father stood up and wiped his greasy hands on a dirty rag. "I guess things are all cluttered," he said. "Why don't you get that box out back and we'll both get rid of this junk."

Keith grinned, "It worked, God. Thank You!"

Hide and Seek Words ☐

As you read your Bible try to find these hidden words:

"Charity [love] . . . Is not easily provoked"

Love Doesn't Get Angry Easily

"Hi!" Keith said as he sat down in the living room with his parents. He picked up a magazine and started looking through it. He tried to remember the last time he had sat there in that room with them. His thoughts were suddenly interrupted by his father saying, "Well, well, our little 'goody-goody' has come to sit with us."

Keith's throat went dry as the familiar teasing pricked his heart. Quietly he got up and walked out of the room. "Good night," he called as he went upstairs to his room. His parents watched him leave.

"You shouldn't have been so hard on him," whispered his mother. "He's trying so hard. He didn't even blow up just now. He usually gets so angry when you say something like that to him."

Keith's father shook his head and said, "He certainly is different."

Hide and Seek Words ☐

As you read your Bible try to find these hidden words:

"Charity [love] . . . thinketh no evil"

Love Doesn't Think Bad Things

Keith was glad he felt no hatred toward his parents. But he wasn't sure how he should feel about their cruelty to him. His love-order from God said not to think about bad things.

Keith reasoned, "When I keep thinking about something bad that's happened, it seems to get worse and I get more upset. I guess I'll just have to stop thinking about it. Maybe I should try to understand why they act the way they do. Or, maybe I should just figure that they don't really mean what they say."

Keith sighed, "Even if I can't figure out why they act as they do, or even if they do mean what they say, I can't think about it. If I do, it will just hurt me more. If I let them hurt me, I'll start hating them again and I want to love them."

Hide and Seek Words ☐

As you read your Bible try to find these hidden words:

"Charity [love] . . . rejoiceth in the truth"

Love Looks for Good Things

Keith decided, *I'm going to obey God's love-order that says to think about good things. I'm going to love my folks no matter what.*

Just before bedtime Keith clumped downstairs for a snack. "Want anything?" he called to his parents as he stuck his head in the refrigerator.

"Not now," answered his father. His parents watched as he whistled his way back upstairs with a huge chicken and pickle sandwich.

"Good night," Keith called back to them.

"He certainly is different," said his mother. "Usually he's so unfriendly and suspicious. I always feel guilty about him because . . . I know we aren't as nice . . . as we could be."

Keith's father walked over to his wife. "Maybe we could use a little changing ourselves," he said.

Hide and Seek Words ☐

As you read your Bible try to find these hidden words:

"Charity [love] . . . never faileth"

Love Lasts

" . . . And that's it!" finished Keith. His cheeks were red with excitement as he told his parents everything he'd learned about the Lord Jesus and love. He's real and His love lasts forever. I can't explain it, but I know it's true!"

"You are certainly changed," whispered Keith's mother. "I wish I dared to believe God could change me too."

Keith was excited! "God can if you ask Him to. He loves you and wants to forgive your sin. You can't change yourself, but God can!"

Keith's father put one arm around his wife and the other around his son, then bowed his head. "God," he prayed, "We are sorry for the way we've treated one another and for the way we've treated You. Thank You for loving us and for sending Your Son to die for our sin. Forgive our sin. And . . . take over in each of our lives and in our home. Help us to learn more about how to love You and each other."

Keith's gift of love from God had helped his parents find God.

God's family

© PMi

Hide and Seek Words ☐

As you read your Bible try to find these hidden words:

"He that . . . believeth . . . hath everlasting life"

God's Big Family

Nearly two thousand years ago the Lord Jesus made the wonderful promise in our Hide and Seek words. Ever since that time all those who believe Jesus died to take away their sins and have received Him as their Savior have been born into God's family.

Just think! If you are a Christian, you belong to the same family that believers through all those years belong to—God's family! If you have not asked Jesus to take away your sins, do it right now. Tell Him you're sorry for your sins. Ask Him to save you and He will. Then you, too, will belong to God's big family. All the promises you will read in this little book can be yours!

Hide and Seek Words ☐

As you read your Bible try to find these hidden words:

"...the gift of God is eternal life"

Two Kinds of Water

In the eastern country where Jesus lived, water was very precious. In some villages a water carrier moved up and down the streets with a leather bottle and a cup, selling water. "Buy the gift of God," he cried. Sometimes a rich man might buy the whole bottle and then that man would cry. "The gift of God is free!" How the people hurried to fill their water jugs.

One day Jesus sat by a well and talked with a sinful woman. She came for water to quench her thirst, but Jesus told her of another kind of water. He said that if she drank it she would never be thirsty again. It was a free gift. Our Hide and Seek words tell us this gift of God is_____.

The woman believed Jesus' words and received the gift of eternal life. She was saved from her sins. Have you received God's gift of life eternal? If so, you are in God's family.

Hide and Seek Words □

As you read your Bible try to find these hidden words:

" . . . the whole family . . . is named"

What's Your Name?

Did you ever wonder why those who have believed on the Lord Jesus are called *Christians*? Acts 11:26 tells us that believers were first called *Christians* in the city of Antioch in the land of Syria. This was long ago. The word almost says "Christ-ones," doesn't it? What a good name it is, one we should be proud to have.

The little song, "Red, brown, yellow, black and white, they are precious in His sight," is true. There are Christians just about everywhere in the world. Our verse today tells us that even those who have died and gone to Heaven have this wonderful family name.

Let us do those things that please God so our lives will match our family name. Do others know you are a Christian?

Hide and Seek Words ☐

As you read your Bible try to find these hidden words:

" . . . I will never leave thee"

Five-Finger Exercise

A blind boy learned about the Lord Jesus in his Sunday school class and received Him as his Savior. After his teacher fully explained what it meant to be a Christian, she said, "Hold up your hand." He did and she asked, "How many fingers do you have?" "Five," he replied. Then she told him a most important truth. "Your hand will remind you of the Lord Jesus' special promise, 'I will never leave thee.' There is a word for each finger."

During church the teacher sat next to the blind boy. She watched as he quietly touched each finger of his hand over and over again. He was remembering that Jesus would never leave him.

If you have received Jesus as your Savior He will never leave you either. He has promised to be with you always, all your days. You will never be alone.

Hide and Seek Words ☐

As you read your Bible try to find these hidden words:

"The Lord is my helper"

Help!

One night Lisa prayed by her bed, "Lord Jesus, make me gooder and gooder till there is no bad left." Her mother was listening to her prayer. When Lisa climbed into bed her mother said, "You did the right thing by telling the Lord that you wanted to be good, for He is the only one who can help you."

Did you know the Lord has promised to help *you?* We find these good words in Isaiah 41:10, "I will strengthen *thee;* yea, I will help *thee.*" But

you must allow the Lord to do this. Lisa's way was the best. She prayed and asked Him to help her.

Ask the Lord to help you today. He will!

Hide and Seek Words ☐

As you read your Bible try to find these hidden words:

" . . . happy is the man whom God correcteth"

Strange Happiness

Have you ever said to your mother or dad right after you have been punished for being naughty, "Thank you. That makes me real happy!"

Of course you haven't. But you aren't happy doing wrong things, either, are you? You may not feel happy while you are being punished, but when you do right you are happy. Behaving as you should brings happiness. That's what your Hide and Seek words mean today.

How does God correct you? Often He uses your parents, sometimes a teacher in school, many times a Sunday school teacher or pastor.

When you listen to them and do as they say, you are really obeying God and this makes you happy. Remember this today when someone makes you behave!

Hide and Seek Words ☐

As you read your Bible try to find these hidden words:

"My peace I give unto you"

A Present from Jesus to You

John's parents were getting a divorce and his father was going to live in another city. John was sad, for he loved his father very much. His Sunday school teacher knew how he felt and told him about the disciples.

Jesus had told them He was going to leave them to die on the cross. Then He said something that made them glad. "My peace I give unto you."

"John," said his teacher, "You are God's child. His peace can be yours too."

John thought about it. "Well, I guess if Jesus can give me peace on the *inside,* it won't matter so much what happens on the *outside.*"

Aren't you glad that Jesus never goes back on His promises? When *you* need His peace He will give it to you.

Hide and Seek Words ☐

As you read your Bible try to find these hidden words:

"...let the peace of God rule"

Who's the Umpire?

One of the most important people at a ball game is—have you guessed it?—the umpire! He sees to it that everyone plays fair. He calls the plays. He is the "boss" of the whole game.

Our Hide and Seek words tell us of a heavenly umpire who will keep us from sinning, from making wrong decisions. This umpire is God's peace. This is how it works. You cannot disobey and have peace in your heart if you are in God's family. You cannot go to a place where Christians should not go and still have peace in your heart. If you are troubled inside you need to ask yourself, "Have I done wrong?"

Remember, if you should want to do something bad ask God to help you not to. Let peace rule your life today!

Hide and Seek Words ☐
As you read your Bible try to find these hidden words:
"I will . . . lay me down . . . and sleep"

Go to Sleep!

"You're too big a girl to have a light on in your room all night," said Gina's mother.

"But I get scared in the dark," Gina answered.

Have you ever been afraid when you were alone? David the psalmist said that when he was afraid *he prayed* (Psalm 3:4, 5) and then just laid down and went to sleep. Again he said, "I have set the Lord always before me" (Psalm 16:8). This means he thought about the Lord.

Do you belong to God? Do you pray before you go to sleep? Do you think about the Lord Jesus? Do you remember that He is always near? Then you can go right to sleep!

Hide and Seek Words ☐

As you read your Bible try to find these hidden words:

"...making melody in your heart"

A Singing Heart

Making melody *in your heart* seems like a strange thing to say. Perhaps you think the words should be "*making melody with your voice.*" But the best song of all is the song in our hearts.

In a town across the sea there was an old church which had a great organ. The caretaker was warned never to let anyone play it. One day a stranger came into the church and asked if he could play the organ. "Oh, no!" said the caretaker. But the visitor begged, and finally was allowed to play. Never had the organ sounded so beautiful! The caretaker asked the man his name. "I am Mendelssohn," said the stranger. Mendelssohn was one of the world's greatest musicians!

Your heart is like that organ. When God lives in you, you can have a singing heart. God gives joy to His children.

Hide and Seek Words ☐

As you read your Bible try to find these hidden words:

" . . . his ears are open"

God Listens!

Bill had a problem that he thought was serious. He went to his mother to talk to her about it, but she said, "Bill, I have to go to a meeting right now. Maybe later." He asked his dad if he had a minute to talk with him, but just then his dad was busy fixing his car, and he said, "Can it wait till after lunch?"

Bill was discouraged. He needed someone to talk to who would listen *right then*. Have you ever had this experience? Did you know that the Bible tells us that *God's ears are always open to hear us when we pray?* He is never too busy. No problem is too small. The Bible doesn't lie. You can depend on it—God will listen to your prayer!

Hide and Seek Words ☐
As you read your Bible try to find these hidden words:

"My presence shall go with thee"

Don't Be Afraid!

Mary's family had to move to another city and Mary did not want to go. She would miss her home, her grandma and grandpa, her friends, her Sunday school teacher. She knew she would be lonely. When her mother came to say goodnight, Mary was crying.

"I think we should read a verse in the Bible," said her mother, who understood why Mary was sad. Together they read, "And, behold, I am with thee, and will keep thee in all places whither thou goest" (Genesis 28:15). "You see, Mary," said her mother, "no matter where we go, the *Lord* has promised to be with us. This verse also says that He will *keep* us ... He can even keep us from loneliness!" Mary felt much better.

Aren't you glad that Jesus has promised to be with *all* of His family no matter where they live?

Hide and Seek Words ☐

As you read your Bible try to find these hidden words:

"...clean hands"

Look At Your Hands!

There are two kinds of stains we get on our hands. The first kind comes off and the second doesn't. The first we get when we play in the dirt, or dig in the garden, or change a bicycle tire. A good scrub with soap and water takes care of these hands. The second is the "stain" we can't see. It is when we do something mean or dishonest.

Take a good look at your hands. Do they steal? Are they sometimes greedy? Are they ever cruel? Our verses today tell us nobody is fit for God's presence with hands that have sinned. No amount of scrubbing on our part can cleanse away sin. But God can! He will give us clean hands and a pure heart if we ask Him.

Don't let today go by without asking the Lord Jesus to cleanse you from sin.

Hide and Seek Words ☐

As you read your Bible try to find these hidden words:

"**. . . keep thy tongue**"

Watch It!

Here is a puzzle: *What is small and hidden, but a very important part of your head?*

Your tongue is so important, the Bible speaks of it 152 times! Never think what you say is a small thing! Your words either hurt or help. A tongue that pleases God knows when to be quiet and when to speak. It doesn't blurt out whatever comes to your mind. It doesn't just chatter. A *true* tongue never tells a lie. It knows that it is far better to suffer for telling the truth than to escape punishment by lying. A *pure* tongue never swears, never repeats bad stories. A *kind* tongue never picks out faults of others and talks about them. Rather, it tries to find good things to say. It cheers and comforts and doesn't make others miserable.

Are you in God's family? Then what do you say with *your* tongue?

Hide and Seek Words ☐

As you read your Bible try to find these hidden words:

" . . . **confess . . . he is
faithful . . . to forgive**"

Unhappy Hiding

Do you remember how Adam and Eve were afraid after they had sinned and tried to hide from God? They were like children who hide behind their fingers thinking their mother won't see them. But they could not hide from God!

Have you ever done something wrong and thought no one would ever find out? You may hide your sin from others, but God knows all about you. This need not frighten you. All the time Adam and Eve were trying to hide, God was really seeking them out, longing for them to confess their sin and be forgiven.

When you feel afraid of God that is not the time to run away *from* Him. It is exactly the time to go to Him in prayer. Do not be foolish like Adam and Eve. Take your sin to God instead. He will forgive and cleanse you.

Hide and Seek Words ☐

As you read your Bible try to find these hidden words:

"... **the word is ... in thy ... heart**"

Happy Hiding

"I don't see any use in learning Bible verses," said John. "I just forget them again!"

"You're wrong there," said Dave. "If we hide God's Word in our hearts it will keep us from sinning. That's a promise, and God always keeps His promises." (If you don't think so, read Psalm 119:11.)

Yes, Dave was right. You may think you have forgotten the verses, but just when you need them they will come to your mind. It is important to learn as many verses as you can, then all through your life they will be ready to help you. And did you ever think about helping somebody else with the words you have learned? You can!

Hide and Seek Words ☐

As you read your Bible try to find these hidden words:

"Follow peace"

Don't Pick a Fight!

Quarreling is an easy thing to do. Sometimes easier than *not* quarreling. Even the disciples of Jesus had this problem. They argued about who was the greatest disciple. Does this seem strange to you? It shouldn't, for people are just the same today as they have always been.

Sometimes boys and girls quarrel because they are touchy. The tiniest problem causes a quarrel. Sometimes quarreling comes because we want our own way and won't give in. But the biggest reason for quarrels is selfishness. If you want something that someone else has it's far

better to give it up than to lose your temper and start a quarrel.

When you are in God's family it's your *business* to keep from quarreling. 1 Peter 3:11 tells us two

things to do: Look for peace and then run after it! You can't do this and have a quarrel!

Hide and Seek Words ☐

As you read your Bible try to find these hidden words:

"I am the bread of life"

What Is It?

"We are hungry!" complained the children of Israel to Moses, their leader. They had been wandering in the wilderness with no place to buy food. Moses asked God about it and God sent them food from Heaven. When they saw the small round pieces covering the ground each morning, they said, "Manna," which in the Hebrew language means "What is it?"

Manna is a beautiful picture of the Lord Jesus Christ. He came down from Heaven to bring life to the real you—your spirit. He is the *living* Bread. When you receive Him as your Savior from sin you receive everlasting life.

Manna was in reach of everyone and did not cost anything. Jesus died for everyone. He is God's free gift to you and me. Have you accepted God's gift? Then why not tell someone else this story today so they can know that Jesus will forgive their sin and give them new life too.

Hide and Seek Words ☐

As your read your Bible try to find these hidden words:

" . . . guide me"

Do You Know the Way?

John's father was working in another part of town. One day he asked John to bring him his lunch. He left a note telling him exactly how to get there. When noon came John picked up the lunch his mother had fixed, but left the note on the kitchen table.

"I know the way myself," he said. He started out, but took a wrong turn, then another, and soon he was hopelessly lost. How he wished he had that note with the directions!

How silly of him, but you may be as foolish as John! God has given you a guide to keep you on the right way. It is the Bible. Do you read it every day? Do you do what it says? God has promised He will guide you through His Word until you get to Heaven. Don't neglect to read your directions!

Hide and Seek Words ☐

As you read your Bible try to find these hidden words:

"Good . . . medicine"

Strange Medicine

When you think of medicine you probably think of hard-to-swallow pills or bad-tasting liquid. But our Hide and Seek words speak of a different kind of medicine—a happy heart.

A merry heart is good for yourself. You feel better, so you do better work in school. It helps you to make the best of things. A merry heart sees fun in all sorts of situations. It even makes you *look* better, (if you don't believe it, read Proverbs 15:13.)

A merry heart is good for others. When you take medicine you expect it to help you, but not the girl or boy next door. But this strange medicine, a merry heart, is good for everybody! No one likes to be around a grumpy, out-of-sorts person. But everyone likes to be near a happy one.

Shouldn't God's children be the happiest in the world?

Hide and Seek Words ☐

As you read your Bible try to find these hidden words:

". . . for the master's use"

Ready for Action!

You aren't very big or very old. Have you ever wondered if God can use you?

The Bible tells us that God wants to use everybody in His family. We are called "dishes," which is what the word "vessels" means in our verses today. (Did you read them?) We carry the Gospel, God's wonderful message of salvation. No matter who we are, God who is our master will use us to help others. All He asks is that we be clean. This does not mean scrubbed with soap (although this is important too). It means we should live so that we are pure and good and honorable.

God will use you to help others if you are willing and if you refuse to do what is unkind or wrong.

Hide and Seek Words ☐

As you read your Bible try to find these hidden words:

"...love one another"

Loving Is Giving

John 3:16 tells us that God showed His love to us by giving His Son to die on the cross for our sins. For those in God's family, loving is shown by giving, too.

There are different ways of giving. Loving is giving *in*. Two girls were sitting on a high stool that was too small for them. Sally said to Jane, "If one of us got down there would be more room for me!" When two people want the same thing, one of them has to give in. How often do *you* give in?

Loving is giving *up*. John had a pet canary that he loved. His mother was very ill. One day John saw a look of pain cross her face when the canary chirped his shrill song. Without saying a word John took the canary and cage and gave them to his cousin.

How do *you* show love?

Hide and Seek Words ☐

As you read your Bible try to find these hidden words:

"... ye have done it unto me"

Loving Is Doing

Jimmy had only been saved a little while.

"I wish Jesus lived on earth right now," he said to his mother, "because I would like to do something for Him to show Him I love Him."

"You can do something to show Him," said his mother. She got out the snow shovel and explained, "Here, you go and shovel Mrs. Smith's walk for her."

"How will that be showing Jesus I love Him?" asked Jimmy.

"Son, remember that when you do something kind for someone because you love Jesus, it's the same as doing it for Jesus. You can do special things for Jesus every day."

Jimmy was glad to know this, and hurried down the street with the snow shovel over his shoulder.

Hide and Seek Words ☐

As you read your Bible try to find these hidden words:

" . . . think on these things"

A Peep into Your Mind

There is a little game boys and girls sometimes play. One person thinks of an object and the others try to guess what is in his mind by asking questions.

Have you ever asked yourself, "What are my thoughts like?" If they were flashed on television, would you care? Or would you be ashamed? Did you know your thoughts tell what you are really like? Both what you do and what you say comes from your thoughts.

If a dirty or hateful thought comes into your mind, you don't have to let it stay. Ask God to take it away. Count the things God has told you to think about in your verse today. Think on these things and there won't be room for bad thoughts!

Hide and Seek Words ☐

As you read your Bible try to find these hidden words:

"... worship the Lord"

Do You Worship?

Three questions today: *What is worship?* Do you remember when the wise men came from the East to worship the newborn King Jesus? What did they do? They gave Him wonderful gifts. When we worship God we give Him the best that we have—our hearts and lives. We praise Him. We

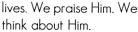

think about Him.

Where should we worship? Perhaps you say, "I can worship anywhere." God also tells us to worship in His house. David, the psalmist said, "I *will* come into thy house... in thy fear will I worship" (Psalm 5:7). He was determined that nothing would keep him from worshiping in God's house. God wants us to worship Him each week in church with other Christians.

How should we worship? The Bible tells us we should worship quietly and reverently (Psalm 29:2). Is this how you worship?

Hide and Seek Words ☐

As you read your Bible try to find these hidden words:

" . . . deliver us from evil"

Catching Birds

The Indian had a clever way of catching birds. He placed a kernel of corn in plain view, tied a loop of his own hair around it, then

lay flat on the ground holding the hair. When a bird landed to eat the corn, he pulled the hair and it snapped tight around the bird's leg. What a clever way to snare a bird by this "fowler" (the word for bird catcher).

Did you know that Satan has clever ways to catch you and cause you to sin? Today he may tempt you to steal, to lie, to cheat, to disobey. But listen to God's promises: "Surely he [God] shall deliver thee from the snare of the fowler [the devil]" (Psalm 91:3). God has promised to help you and deliver you from evil. You don't have to be caught!

Hide and Seek Words □

As you read your Bible try to find these hidden words:

" . . . **we ought to obey**"

Who Obeys God?

The disciples of the Lord Jesus were put in prison for telling people how Jesus could save them from their sins. When an angel let them out, right away they went to the temple and began to teach the people. This made the ruler angry, and he sent for them.

"Didn't I give you strict orders not to teach about Jesus?" he shouted.

Even though they knew the ruler might put them back in prison or maybe even kill them, the disciples were determined to do what Jesus had told them to do. Bravely they said, *"We ought to obey God rather than men."*

You may never be put in prison for obeying, but you may be made fun of or criticized when you witness for Jesus. Do you obey God?

Hide and Seek Words □

As you read your Bible try to find these hidden words:

" . . . a place for you"

Heaven

Sarah's best friend was dead and Sarah was very sad. She loved Julie very much. They had such good times together. Now Julie was gone and Sarah couldn't understand why.

"Let's talk about it," said mother. "We know that Julie had received the Lord Jesus Christ as her own Savior, don't we?"

"Yes, I know she is in Heaven. But Heaven seems so far away and I don't know much about it."

Then her mother explained, "The Bible tells us wonderful things about Heaven. Best of all, Jesus is there and Julie is with Him. This is 'far better' than anything we can imagine (Philippians 1:23). Julie suffered so much and there is no pain there."

"I'm glad Julie is in Heaven with Jesus after all," Sarah decided.

Hide and Seek Words ☐

As you read your Bible try to find these hidden words:

"The Lord taketh pleasure"

You Can Make God Happy!

Can you think of some of the things you have learned in this little book that make you happy? God is with you. He protects you from harm. His ears are always open to hear you pray. He is preparing a place for you in Heaven. And oh, so many more!

But did you know that *you* can make *God* happy? You can! When you fear Him, He is happy. Does this mean that you should be scared of God? Of course not. The word "fear" in this verse means to "trust with respect." When you trust in the Lord with all your heart, He is glad. Don't try to work things out by yourself today. Trust the Lord Jesus to help you. When it's hard to behave trust Him to help you. When you are afraid, trust Him. When you don't feel like praying, ask Him to help you. You will be happy—and God will be happy too!

Hide and Seek Words ☐

As you read your Bible try to find these hidden words:

"**...born again...by the word of God**"

Two Families

Did you ever feel that maybe you weren't a Christian after all? You just cannot seem to keep from doing bad things. And you know that you displease the Lord by the way you behave. Are you still in God's family? The answer is easy.

Are you still a part of your own family when you are bad? You were *born* into your earthly family, and nothing can change that. So it is in your heavenly family. When you are born into God's family, you belong to God forever. You are safe.

Of course *this doesn't mean that you can do just as you please!* God hates sin. You must ask Him to forgive you when you sin. (Read 1 John 1:9 again.) You need to pray and read God's Word every day to help you stop sinning.

Living in God's family

Hide and Seek Words ☐

As you read your Bible try to find these hidden words:

"... **be born again**"

Born Into God's Family

Leo the Lion is a puppet. He tells the children he wants to be an Indian! First, he puts on a feathered headband. Does *that* make him an Indian? No! Then he learns some Indian words. Does *that* make him an an Indian? Of course not!

We say, "Leo, to be an Indian you must be born an Indian!"

Leo reminds me of some people I know. They try to be Christians by being good. But to be a Christian you must be born into God's family. God's Son, Jesus Christ, died for your sin so that you could be accepted by God who has no sin. You must believe He did this for you and pray something like this...

"Dear Jesus, please forgive the wrong things I've done and be my Savior from sin."

That's how you become a Christian. Have *you* been born into God's family?

Hide and Seek Words □

As you read your Bible try to find these hidden words:

"Suffer [let] little children . . . come"

Not Too Young

Some people think you have to wait until you're grown up to be born again into God's family. But, that's not true. Children need to be born into God's family too.

One day when Jesus was teaching the people, His disciples tried to keep the children from bothering Him.

But Jesus said, "Let the children come unto Me. Don't send them away."

Jesus loves children. He loves you. He does not think you are bothering Him when you come to Him and talk to Him.

He just wants you to ask Him to be your Savior. Then He wants you to bring your problems to Him. He is *never* too busy for *you!*

Come little children
Come unto Me.
I want to be your friend
Throughout eternity.

Hide and Seek Words ☐

As you read your Bible try to find these hidden words:

**"...desire the...word
...that ye may grow"**

God's Word—Our Food

We have a teenager in our house. He has such big feet we call him, "Timmy the Toes," or "Freddie the Foot"!

Your mother probably says to you when you have outgrown some of your clothes, "Won't you ever stop growing?" But your mom and dad would feel pretty bad if you did not grow. When babies do not grow their parents take them to a doctor to find out what is wrong. It is sad to see a baby who is not growing because that means he is sick.

When you are born into God's family He

wants to see you grow too. Your body grows when you feed it good food. You grow to be like Jesus by "feeding" on (reading) God's Word.

Read God's Word every day so you may grow strong in the Lord.

Hide and Seek Words ☐
As you read your Bible try to find these hidden words:

" . . . pray one for another"

Who Needs Your Prayers?

Tim was baby-sitting eight-year-old Ryan.

"Tim, are you afraid to die?" Ryan asked. Tim explained that he had received Jesus as his Savior from sin and so he wasn't afraid of nuclear power and death and many other things which frightened Ryan. He invited Ryan to ask Jesus to be his Savior too. And Ryan did. Ryan sighed a sigh of relief after he prayed, "Now I feel better already," he said. He knew Jesus was with him so he didn't have to be afraid anymore.

But Ryan's mother stopped calling for Tim to baby-sit. She said Ryan didn't need Jesus.

Ryan is like a new baby with no one to feed him. He needs a Christian friend in his neighborhood or at school to help him grow in Jesus.

Do you know someone like Ryan who needs your help? Ask Jesus to show you someone who needs you to help him grow.

Hide and Seek Words ☐

As you read your Bible try to find these hidden words:

"How sweet are thy words"

Sharing In God's Word

Janet read her Sunday school paper on Sunday afternoon and then tossed it into the wastebasket like she always did. Suddenly she thought about her friend Jennifer. Jenny's parents would not let her go to Sunday school. *Maybe she could learn about Jesus by reading my Sunday school papers,* Janet thought. She got the paper out of the wastebasket and slipped it into her notebook. Tomorrow at school she would give it to Jenny.

Jenny looked forward to reading the stories in the papers each Monday during lunchtime. Later she told Janet, "I had asked Jesus to be my Savior one day when my grandmother prayed with me. But after Grandma died I had no one to talk to about Jesus."

Now with the Sunday school papers to read and a friend like Janet to talk to, Jenny could begin to grow in the Lord.

Hide and Seek Words ☐

As you read your Bible try to find these hidden words:

"Be . . . an example"

Spring Fever

Jim and Robbie had been best friends since kindergarten. They both received the Lord Jesus at Mrs. Mills' Good News Club.™ One warm day near the end of May Jim said, "Hey Robbie, some of the other kids are going to skip school tomorrow and go to Peter's Pond to fish. Let's go too!"

"I don't think we better," Robbie said.

"Oh, come on. It'll be fun and it's just too hot to stay in school. Some of the guys said they did it last year and they didn't get into trouble."

"It's not that, Jim, I just don't think Jesus would want us to," Robbie answered.

"Yeah, you're right. I hadn't thought about how He would feel!"

The next day after school the boys were walking home together.

"You know, Robbie, "it was a fun day in school today. Besides, I feel good knowing we obeyed the Lord!"

Hide and Seek Words ☐

As you read your Bible try to find these hidden words:

"Love your enemies . . . do good to them"

Break That Circle

"Suzie is the meanest girl in school," Sharon complained to her mother. "She's really mean!"

"Why don't you try being nice to her," Mother suggested.

"Nice to her! Who wants to be nice to her, everybody hates her, Mother!" Sharon exclaimed.

Sharon's mother explained, "The meaner people are to Suzie, the meaner she will be in return. It's like an evil circle. Someone must break that circle, Sharon. Why don't you let Jesus use you to do it?"

It wasn't easy but Sharon took her mother's advice. She saw Suzie walking ahead of her on her way to school.

"Suzie, wait for me. I'll walk with you to school."

That was just the beginning. The nicer Sharon was to Suzie, the nicer Suzie was to her. It took a while, but Suzie actually promised to go to Sunday school with Sharon the next Sunday.

Hide and Seek Words ☐

As you read your Bible try to find these hidden words:

"Christ . . . strengtheneth me"

Habits

As Mr. Smith wound thread around Sam's outstretched hands, he asked, "Did you ever notice how habits become stronger with time?" Mr. Smith was talking to the kids at camp. He wound just a few threads around Sam's hands at first. "There, see if you can break that, Sam," he said. With little effort Sam broke the threads.

Next time a few more threads were added. It took more strength, but Sam did pop the threads.

Again more layers of thread were added. Sam tried but this time he could not break them.

"That's just like a bad habit," Mr. Smith pointed out. The longer you do it, the harder it is to stop it. It's best not to start a bad habit, but if you are already "tied up" by one, ask the Lord Jesus to help you break it.

Bad habits sometimes make it hard for others to love us. They can also cause unhappiness in the family of God.

Hide and Seek Words ☐

As you read your Bible try to find these hidden words:

" . . . the whole family in heaven"

What a Big Family!

Shelly was an only child. When she was little she thought she heard her mother telling people she was a "lonely child." *How true*, she thought. *To be an only child is to be a lonely child.*

One Sunday morning Shelly sat leaning against her mother's arm in church. She wasn't listening very carefully until she heard the pastor say, "You must be born into the family of God to have eternal life."

Shelly sat up straight. *I do have brothers and sisters*, she thought. *Most of the kids in my*

Sunday school class have been born again so they're my brothers and sisters in God's family. That's neat, I'll never call myself an "only" child again and I sure never need to be a lonely child!

Hide and Seek Words ☐

As you read your Bible try to find these hidden words:

" . . . preferring one another"

You First

It was spring and Uncle Jim had just given Billy and Bobby each money to buy a kite. The boys were excited as they ran to the toy shop. They hurried to the shelf where the kites had been stacked. There was one left! Bobby thought for a minute and then said, "Go ahead, Billy, you can have it."

"Thanks a lot, Bob," his brother said as he happily grabbed the last kite.

"That was nice of you to put your brother first," said the clerk, "Let me look out back and see if our new shipment of kites came in."

Sure enough they had, but they were bigger and more expensive. "Bobby, you can have one of these for the same price since you were so kind."

Now, putting others first does not mean you will always get the best at that moment. But, God will bless you for obeying His word.

Hide and Seek Words ☐

As you read your Bible try to find these hidden words:

" . . . putting away lying"

I Lied!

Chris and Dave went to the same church. They also went to the same school. David was a real athlete and very popular at school. Chris was a bookworm and didn't have too many friends.

"Hey, Dave," Chris asked at school one day, "Do you want to go to the school circus with me on Saturday?"

Dave did not want to go to the circus with Chris! What would the other kids think?

"Uh, sorry, but I already promised Ed I'd go with him," Dave replied.

That evening Dave's dad read from Ephesians for family devotions, "Wherefore, putting away lying, speak every man truth with his neighbor: for we are members one of another."

"Chris and I are both members of God's family and I lied to him," Dave said softly. "I didn't tell Ed I'd go with him. I'm going to call Chris and tell him the truth and offer to go with him."

Hide and Seek Words ☐
As you read your Bible try to find these hidden words:

" . . . **brotherly kindness**"

How Much Is Five Pennies?

"Look what my friend, Mr. Jones, made for me, Tommy," said his little brother, Tad.

"Hey, that's a neat kite, Tad. You want to sell it to me?" Tommy asked.

"OK!" Tad replied. The idea of having some money of his own was too much for little Tad to resist.

"I'll tell you what. You can have these five shiny pennies or these two little dimes. Which do you want?"

If you have a little brother or sister you know which Tad picked—the five shiny pennies. To him it looked like a lot more than two little dimes.

Do you think Tommy cheated his brother? Did he show kindness? Do you think Jesus was pleased with what Tommy did?

Hide and Seek Words ☐

As you read your Bible try to find these hidden words:

"The words of his mouth are . . . deceit"

A Good Idea

"I'm scared," said Stephanie to Marcy as they walked to school. "Our book report is due today and I didn't even read the book!"

"Don't worry, I'll tell you about it."

Stephanie listened well as Marcy told her about the book. She got a B- on her report. But she wasn't happy. She knew what she had to do. She told Marcy.

"Miss Cook," Stephanie sobbed, "I didn't read that book." Then she explained what happened.

"What you girls did was deceitful."

"Deceitful?"

"Yes, that means you tried to cover the truth. But since you are now telling me the truth you will not be punished. Stephanie, you read that book by Friday and write a new report."

"I'm sorry I got you in trouble, Steph."

"That's OK, Marcy. From now on let's help each other not to do things that don't please the Lord."

"Good idea!"

Hide and Seek Words ☐

As you read your Bible try to find these hidden words:

"Love your enemies"

Your Secret Weapon

You have a secret weapon. You can use it to win many battles and never hurt anyone. That weapon is called love!

Do you have a teacher whom you feel does not like you? Ask God to give you a special love for that teacher. Then, show your love by being kind and thoughtful.

Is there a person in your class at school or church who is always mean to you? Be loving and kind to that person. You may be able to help him trust Jesus as his Savior.

The Bible says "love is *always* kind." This does not mean just being kind so you can win others to Jesus. We are to do good "especially to those of the household of faith"—our brothers and sisters in Christ (Galatians 6:10).

Hide and Seek Words ☐

As you read your Bible try to find these hidden words:

"Use hospitality ... without grudging"

Visitors!

"Mrs. Smith is going to have an opera-tion," Mrs. Elms announced at supper one evening. "Cindy and Jenny will be staying with us while their mother is in the hospital."

"Oh, no!" Karen exclaimed.

"They're nothing but trouble," Jeff echoed.

It was Dad's turn to speak up. "Cindy and Jenny were just saved recently. Maybe they just need to grow in the Lord and you could help them. Also, God's Word teaches us to be hospitable which means to treat guests kindly."

This was a new challenge for Karen and Jeff. When their "unwanted" visitors arrived they had a different attitude toward them. Family devotions were more interesting than ever as these guests asked questions and the whole family tried to answer them. Interesting discussions followed.

"We're glad you came," said Karen and Jeff. Cindy and Jenny were glad they had come too.

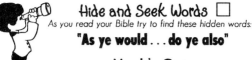

Hide and Seek Words ☐

As you read your Bible try to find these hidden words:

"As ye would . . . do ye also"

Mark's Quiz

"Mom, I know that Bill says he is a Christian, but, if he makes fun of me just one more time, I'm gonna hit him!"

"Mark," Mother asked, "is that the way you would want Bill to treat you? The Lord Jesus said, 'As ye would that men should do to you, do ye also to them.'"

The next morning when Mark sat down to breakfast there was a paper by his plate. It looked like this,

QUIZ

If Bill makes fun of me again I should:
1 Hit him
2 Forgive him
3 Make fun of him
4 Go home and cry
5 Never forgive him

Which answer would you choose? If you chose answer number 2, you were right because that is how the Lord Jesus wants you to treat others.

Hide and Seek Words ☐

As you read your Bible try to find these hidden words:

"Weep with them that weep"

How to Win a Friend for Jesus

Brian had never received the Lord Jesus as his Savior and he didn't like the twins next door to tell him about sin. In fact, he wanted to be left alone so he could play with his dog, Pal.

One day after school Brian heard brakes screech in front of his house. He ran out and found his dog had been hit. The twins heard too and stood beside Brian as tears rolled down his cheeks. The twins began to cry too as they helped pick Pal up and carried him to the veterinarian down the street. A few minutes later the doctor said that Pal would be all right. He had a few broken bones but he would be fine. The boys jumped up and down for joy.

Then Brian asked, "Why did you help me come here?"

"Because we like you and want to be your friends," the twins answered.

That week the three boys went to Sunday school together.

Hide and Seek Words ☐

As you read your Bible try to find these hidden words:

" . . . **let us do good**"

The Do-Gooders Club

Mrs. Dean gave out the memory verse for the week. It was, " . . . do good unto all men, especially unto them who are of the household of faith."

"I've got an idea," said Jeff. "Let's start a 'Do-Gooders Club'!"

"A 'Do-Gooders Club'?" Jerry looked puzzled.

"Yes, we'll do good things for people, especially people in God's family, like our verse said."

"Let's start by mowing Mrs. Perkins' lawn after school tomorrow."

"What a thoughtful thing for you boys to do," Mrs. Perkins said as she served cookies to the boys when they finished her lawn. "I have no one to help me and I do get so lonely."

The boys were talking on their way home. "Those stories Mrs. Perkins told about the old days sure were interesting."

"Yeah, I think I'm going to like this 'Do-Gooders Club'."

Hide and Seek Words ☐

As you read your Bible try to find these hidden words:

"I was sick, and ye visited me"

Letters of Joy

"Bobby Brown is in the hospital," Mrs. Brent announced, "I think we should all visit him."

"But, kids aren't allowed into the hospital," the children objected.

"That's true, but you can visit Bobby with letters."

"Oh, no," they all moaned. "We hate to write letters!"

"I don't even write to my sick grandmother—that's how much I hate to write," Steve added.

But Steve felt restless that night. What if *he* was in the hospital with nothing to do all day? What if he lived alone like his grandmother? That did it! Steve prayed, "Lord, help me to do what I don't want to do, for Jesus' sake."

Letter writing became a regular part of Steve's hobbies and to his surprise it brought *him* joy to bring this joy to others.

Hide and Seek Words □

As you read your Bible try to find these hidden words:

"...a soft answer"

Don't Argue?

In Sunday school we talked about how to win our families to Jesus.

"Be helpful," someone suggested.

"Share," said another.

"Be kind," someone else said.

"These are great ideas. But how about stopping an argument which your brother or sister starts?"

One girl spoke up, "You just don't know my sister—she's so mean!"

"Is she a Christian?"

"No."

"Are you?"

"Yes."

"Shouldn't you be the one to stop the argument then?"

What means more to you, winning others to Jesus or winning an argument?

Think about it!

I'm glad I'm a part of the family of God,
Saved from my sins through His precious blood.
But what about those I meet on my way,
Will they see Jesus in my life today?

Hide and Seek Words ☐

As you read your Bible try to find these hidden words:

"...but are helpers"

Helpful Hannah

Kelly was discouraged. She had received the Lord Jesus as her Savior but her parents were not saved. Kelly's mother and dad were going to get divorced and there were many fights at home.

Hannah was Kelly's friend. She wondered how she could help her. So she made a list of ideas.

HANNAH'S LIST
1. Pray for Kelly.
2. Pray for her parents.
3. Tell Kelly I'm praying for her.
4. Be a very good friend.
5. Encourage her to come to church.
6. Get a Bible for her to read.

That's a pretty good list. Can you think of other ideas? Do you know a friend in God's family who needs *you*?

Hide and Seek Words ☐

As you read your Bible try to find these hidden words:

" . . . all one in Christ Jesus"

No Difference

Sharon couldn't keep from staring at the new girl in class. She was so different. Her eyes were slanted and her skin was dark. Not real dark, but darker than Sharon's own skin. The new girl's name was Kim.

At lunch time Kim walked shyly up to Sharon. "You want to play hop-scotch?" she asked. Kim and Sharon played all lunch hour. *Kim's really not so different after all,* Sharon thought.

It is the same with our brothers and sisters in God's family. They come from every race. The Bible tells us in Galatians 3:28 that there is no difference between Jews and Gentiles, slaves or free men, but by faith we are all one in Christ.

It matters not if your skin is dark,

Or your eyes are brown, green or blue.

If Jesus lives within your heart,

Then you're in God's family, too!

Hide and Seek Words ☐

As you read your Bible try to find these hidden words:

"... all things are become new"

New Girl

Sue and Cindy were walking home from Good News Club.™ Cindy had asked Jesus to be her Savior just a few weeks ago in club.

"You know, Cindy, it seems funny to me, but at the beginning of this year I thought you were a real creep! Now I like you a lot. You must have changed."

Cindy laughed, "No, Sue, I haven't changed. It's just that after you get saved things look different. The things that used to seem important don't seem important anymore. The friends who don't love Jesus, you don't find as interesting. It's because you are born again—a 'new creature' as the Bible says."

"Oh, I see, so you didn't change; I did!"

"Right, and I like the new you, Sue!"

Hide and Seek Words ☐
As you read your Bible try to find these hidden words:

". . . by this shall all men know"

Love Shows the Way

Troy was only in kindergarten but he knew enough about the Bible to know what Jimmy needed.

"You know, Jimmy, you're bad! Why don't you come to my house and let my mommy tell you about Jesus. I used to be bad in nursery school but now I have Jesus in my heart and He helps me."

Troy's teacher overheard the conversation. With tears in her eyes she told Troy's parents, "If Troy is an example of a little boy with Jesus in his heart, maybe that's what Jimmy needs."

Troy showed love for Jimmy. His teacher saw that love.

The Bible says that all men will know we are Christ's disciples (followers) if we love one another. Many teachers have been led to Jesus by their students. Does your teacher see Jesus' love in your life? If your teacher already knows Jesus you can encourage her by being a good example.

Hide and Seek Words ☐

As you read your Bible try to find these hidden words:

"Let patience have her perfect work"

I Want It Yesterday!

"Mom, can I have some ice cream?"

Mother is on the phone and signals for you to hush.

"MOM! I'm starving!"

"Shhh!"

You tug at her, make faces, and stomp your foot.

Does this sound like a scene at *your* house? It sounds like a scene in *many* homes. What sin does this remind you of?

1. Pride
2. Lying
3. Impatience

If you chose number 3, you are right. You can have joy in your family or with others if you are willing to be patient.

Ask God to help you be more patient. It takes prayer and practice!

Here are six unhappy words

As you soon will see.

They are "No!" "Don't!"

And, "you come *after* me."

Hide and Seek Words ☐
As you read your Bible try to find these hidden words:

"Bear ye one another's burdens"

Be a Burden Bearer

Are you a pretty good student in school? If you are, be thankful. Thank God for the gift of a good brain and ask Him to help you use it for Him.

You can start right now to use your brain for God. How?

Do you have a Christian friend who is not doing well in school? The Bible tells us, when one member suffers we all suffer. That means when one member of God's family has a problem we all share that problem.

Help that friend by offering to pray with him and help him learn his spelling or times-tables, or whatever is a problem to him. Help him bear his burden. You'll be glad you did!

Hide and Seek Words ☐

As you read your Bible try to find these hidden words:

"...that ye may be sincere"

Without Wax

I heard a story once about how we got the word *sincere*. Long ago when a potter was making a lovely vase it would sometimes crack. So, rather than destroy the vase and start over, the potter would fill in the crack with wax. You could not see the crack when the vase was finished. But it was not a perfect vase.

When God tells us we should be sincere He means we should be free from impurity or hidden sins (no cracks)!

Do you pretend to be a good Christian at church and then act differently at school? That's not sincere. Ask Jesus to help you be "sincere and without offence [blame] until the day of Christ."

Hide and Seek Words ☐

As you read your Bible try to find these hidden words:

" . . . pray one for another"

Pray!

It was Sunday morning and Pastor Jones was about to pray. Daniel began to wiggle. He looked up at the choir members with their heads bowed. He counted how many men had bald spots.

"Why does Pastor Jones always pray so long!" Daniel said to himself.

What should Daniel have been doing while Pastor Jones prayed? That's right. He should have been praying too! As his pastor prayed for each missionary, Daniel could have been praying—especially for the *children* of the missionaries. If the pastor prayed about something he didn't understand, he could have prayed for a friend, a relative or someone else needing his prayers.

God's Word tells us to pray one for another. We need to be concerned for all of the members of God's wonderful family.

Hide and Seek Words ☐

As you read your Bible try to find these hidden words:

"But to do good and communicate forget not"

Share

God told the Hebrew Christians, "Do good and *communicate*." How would you like to have *that* word—communicate—for a spelling test? It's a great word though. It comes from an old word that means *to share*.

What do you think God wants his family to share?

When you say "Hi" and smile at someone, you communicate. He knows you would like to be his friend.

You can share Christ with others through letters or conversation, even through the way you live.

Remember to communicate for God today.

Hide and Seek Words ☐

As you read your Bible try to find these hidden words:

"...power to become...sons of God"

Are You a Member?

Perhaps you have been reading this little booklet and you're still not sure if you are a member of God's family.

It's easy to know for sure.

First, have you done wrong things? Things you know do not make God happy? We all have, for the Bible tells us that "all have sinned" (Romans 3:23). Your sins keep you out of God's family.

Then, Jesus died for your sins (1 Corinthians 15:3). He did this so you can be a member of His wonderful family.

Ask Jesus to forgive you and receive Him as your Savior. You might pray something like this, "Dear Jesus, I'm sorry for the wrong things I have done. Thank You for dying on the cross for my sins. Thank You that You rose again and are alive today. Please forgive my sins and make me a member of Your family."

friends with God

© PMI

Hide and Seek Words ☐

As you read your Bible try to find these hidden words:

"For God so loved . . . he gave his only . . . Son"

The Perfect Gift

"Hurry and open it, Dad! I hope you like it!" Jim was so excited he could hardly wait for his dad to open the gift he made just for him. It was exactly what dad needed and that made it special. It had cost a lot . . . not money . . . but time. Jim had looked and looked before he found the perfect gift!

God has given you his own very special gift . . . and it's exactly what *you* need. What is it? God's gift to you is His Son, Jesus Christ. God knew you needed Jesus to take the punishment for the wrong things you've said and done. Jesus died for your sins. When you receive God's wonderful gift your sins are forgiven. They no

longer separate you from Him. You can live in friendship with God.

Jesus Christ is the perfect gift from God. Have you received Him?

Hide and Seek Words □

As you read your Bible try to find these hidden words:

" . . . **the friend of God**"

A Special Friend

Have you ever felt lonely when you moved to a new school? You wanted friends . . . but, more than that, you really wanted a special friend.

Special friends like being with you. They play with you at recess and eat with you at lunch . . . even save you a seat! Sometimes you go to each other's homes after school or on the weekends and play games. You can share secrets with a special friend. You can talk over your problems. A special friend listens to you and tries to help you. You can be happy, sad, silly, quiet, or even LOUD with your special friend.

It's good to have friends, but the best friend you can ever have is God! He's always wanted to be a *special* friend to you. He wants to do everything with you. He wants to listen to your secrets and problems and ideas. He wants to be the most wonderful friend you will ever have! Just ask Him!

Hide and Seek Words ☐

As you read your Bible try to find these hidden words:

" . . . **he is faithful . . . to forgive us**"

I'm Sorry

Marci looked at her mom. "I didn't do it!" she said. But in her heart Marci knew she was lying. She had taken the money off the counter. No one saw her . . . or so she thought. She felt ashamed and afraid. Afraid to tell the truth. Afraid of what might happen. On top of that she felt bad about lying to her mom. Even if Mom didn't know, Marci knew she had lied. And she didn't feel right inside anymore. She knew she wouldn't feel right until she told her mother the truth.

Sometimes it's very hard to tell the truth, to admit you were wrong, to say, "I'm sorry." True friends are honest with each other.

You need to be honest with God. You need to say "I'm sorry" when you sin and ask His forgiveness. When you do that, God promises to always forgive you. He also forgets it ever happened! If we confess our sins to Him, He can be depended on to forgive us and to cleanse us from every wrong.

Hide and Seek Words □
As you read your Bible try to find these hidden words:

" . . . I have called you friends"

Loves Me?

Has anyone ever told you, "I love you"? How did it make you feel? Did it make you feel good inside? Safe? Secure? Strong . . . like you could climb the tallest tree or highest building on your block? Don't you like someone to tell you how much they love you again, and again and again?

Do you know how many times and how many ways God tells us He loves us? He tells us over and over again in His Word, the Bible. He loves us so much that He calls us friends. Not only does He tell us He loves us, but He tells us many exciting things about God the Father Himself.

God has chosen to love us . . . just because He wanted to. He has called us to come to Him. If we come to Him by asking the Lord Jesus to be our Savior, we become His friends and He will love us forever.

Hide and Seek Words ☐
As you read your Bible try to find these hidden words:
"I am with you always"

Forever?

How do you know someone wants to be with you? They either ask if you want to do something with them, or if they can be with you. If they like being with you, they'll ask you to come very often or they'll visit you a lot. And if you really like being with someone, you sometimes stay overnight at their house. You want to be with them often, because you have a good time—just being together!

God likes being with you so much that He wants to be with you forever! Yes...forever, always. He wants to share everything you are doing...wherever you go...whatever you do...however you feel. When He comes to live inside you, He promises *never* to leave you. He will be with you forever.

Hide and Seek Words ☐
As you read your Bible try to find these hidden words:
"All Scripture is given...by God"

God's Talk

Some days you can hardly wait to get to school, just so you can talk to your friends. There's always so much to talk about and never enough time. Sometimes it's hard to wait until recess or lunch to talk about what you are going to do after school. Friends talk together about everything.

Your friend, God, likes to talk to you, too. He talks to you through His Word, the Bible. God tells you what He is thinking, what He has done and what He is going to do for you. He tells you how much He loves you. He tells you what makes Him happy and what makes Him sad. He even talks about you in the Bible. He tells about the gifts He has given you.

If you are God's friend, His Holy Spirit lives inside of you. He helps you understand what God says to you in the Bible.

Something to think about: If you do not read your Bible, how will God be able to talk to you?

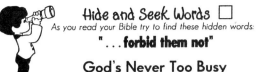

Hide and Seek Words ☐

As you read your Bible try to find these hidden words:

" . . . forbid them not"

God's Never Too Busy

"Hey, Miss Fisher! You want to hear a good riddle?"

"Sorry, Greg, can't right now. I'm too busy."

"Hey, Jamie, listen to this!"

"Can't, Greg, I'm late for my scout meeting."

"Mr. Mitchell, you want to hear a really neat riddle?"

"I've got work to do, Greg. Some other time." No one had time to listen to Greg's riddle!

Have you had something exciting or sad happen that you wanted to tell your friends, but no one had time to listen?

There is someone who is never too busy to listen. That's God. A long time ago, God's Son, Jesus, was talking with some of His friends. Some children came to talk to Jesus and His friends tried to send them away. They didn't think Jesus had time to listen to the children. Jesus was very displeased with what His friends did and He told them, "Let the little children come to talk with me." He wanted to hear what they had to say. Jesus is never too busy to listen!

Hide and Seek Words ☐
As you read your Bible try to find these hidden words:

"...eternal life"

A Special Plan

Debbie was excited. The mailman had brought a letter from her friend Sue. Sue was writing to share her plans for Debbie's visit next week. Sue had made special plans. They would have so much fun!

God has a special plan for us to be with Him. Before you were even born, God knew you would need His plan. God knew you would sin, and so His plan was that His Son, Jesus Christ, would take the punishment you deserve for your sins. Because Jesus died for your sins, you can now be friends with God. If you tell God you are sorry for your sins, and ask Jesus to come into your heart to live, you are God's friend and someday you will live with Him in Heaven forever.

God wants you to be with Him when you leave this earth. He is a wonderful Friend!

Hide and Seek Words ☐
As you read your Bible try to find these hidden words:

"...he hath chosen us"

Need Help?

"Break it up! Miss Morgan is coming!" Jerry was never so happy to see Miss Morgan as he was at that moment. Randy had kept pushing him and calling him names. Jerry had felt himself getting mad. He knew he wasn't supposed to fight, but if Miss Morgan had not come along right then, he didn't know what he would have done.

"Jerry," his teacher said, "I want to help you study for today's spelling test. I know you want to do better on your tests." Jerry felt good. Miss Morgan had not only saved him from getting into trouble for fighting, but she had chosen to help with his schoolwork.

God has chosen to help you to be part of His plans. He has provided the way for you to be saved from the punishment you deserve for your sin. When you tell God you are sorry for your sins He forgives you. He helps you say "no" to sin. Even when you do sin God promises to always forgive you and help you do better if you ask Him to.

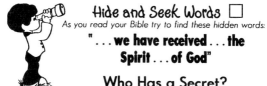

Hide and Seek Words ☐
As you read your Bible try to find these hidden words:

" . . . we have received . . . the Spirit . . . of God"

Who Has a Secret?

Did you ever have a secret? Whom did you share your secret with? Secrets are special messages we sometimes share with our very best friend.

God has secrets, too. He shares His secrets only with His friends . . . those who believe on Him. In fact, there are so many wonderful secrets that God has for His friends that no one can count them all. When you become God's friend He sends His Holy Spirit to tell you all about His wonderful gifts of love.

If you are God's friend you can share your secrets with Him. God knows all things. He

knows every thought you have, but He still wants you to talk about your secrets with Him. He is interested in you!

Hide and Seek Words ☐

As you read your Bible try to find these hidden words:

"...every good gift"

Just What You Need

"Surprise! Happy Birthday!" It was Lauri's birthday and Julie had stopped by to give her a gift. Julie handed Lauri the gift. It was a good gift—something Lauri needed and wanted and Julie wanted to be the one to give it to her. Julie wanted to make Lauri happy. Friends like giving good gifts to each other. It's one way of showing a friend how much you like him and how important he is to you.

God likes giving His friends gifts, too. If you are God's friend, He has some very special gifts for you. His gifts are good because they are just

what you need. Can you guess what some of them are? God will give you His love, His peace, His joy, His kindness, His goodness. He will also give you His gentleness, faithfulness and self control. God gives you His good gifts, so you can be happy. Friends give only good gifts.

Hide and Seek Words □

As you read your Bible try to find these hidden words:

"Trust in him"

What Does It Mean?

What does it mean when you say to a friend, "I trust you"? You probably mean that you can depend on that friend to keep your secrets and to help you when you need it. You can believe that what your friend says is true. A friend doesn't lie to you. He is honest. He keeps his word.

God keeps His word. If you are His friend you can depend on Him. He promises to always be with you, always love you, always forgive you. No matter how big or how little your problems may be, God wants to help you.

God also promises to be a refuge for His friends. What does refuge mean? A refuge is a protection from danger or problems that upset you. God is a friend you can trust and take refuge in.

Hide and Seek Words ☐
As you read your Bible try to find these hidden words:

"I am helped"

Who's Afraid?

Are you ever afraid? Are you afraid of the dark or of being alone? Maybe you're afraid of getting lost. Maybe it's the bully down the street who scares you. Do you ever worry? Do you worry about what's going to happen tomorrow? Do you worry about people liking you? Maybe you worry about something bad happening to your family.

God knows everything you worry about. He knows what you are afraid of. One of God's promises to His friends is that He will help them when they are worried or afraid. All you have to do is ask Him. He will make you strong. He will take away the worry and give you peace inside. Just ask Him. A shield protects someone from harm. God promises to be like a shield for His friends. When you trust in God, He promises to be your strength and shield.

Hide and Seek Words ☐

As your read your Bible try to find these hidden words:

" . . . acquainted with all my ways"

Nobody Understands Me!

Do you know that nothing can be hidden from God? He knows about everyone, everywhere. He knows all about you because He made you. He knows what you are thinking. He knows what you are going to say before you say it. Best of all, He understands you. He knows why you are happy or sad. He knows why your feelings are hurt and why you are angry. He knows why you are afraid. God knows why you act the way you do, and why you say the things you say. God understand you completely. Even when no one else seems to understand you. God does.

Hide and Seek Words ☐

As you read your Bible try to find these hidden words:

"...the Spirit maketh intercession"

Who Prays for You?

"I'll be praying for you, Ginny!" That was the most Janis could do. She didn't know quite what to pray for but it was the only thing she could do to help her friend.

Ginny's parents were divorced and she was going to visit her dad for a few days. It was always upsetting to her. Ginny loved her dad and it hurt not to be with him more. It made her feel better to know that Janis would be praying for her. Janis was a real friend. Ginny knew the Lord Jesus could keep her quiet inside.

God has sent a friend to pray for you—His Holy Spirit. Even when you don't know what to pray for, God's Holy Spirit prays or "makes intercession" for you. You can be sure He will pray for exactly what you need.

Hide and Seek Words ☐

As you read your Bible try to find these hidden words:

"If you lack wisdom . . . ask of God"

God Shares

Jennifer put her pencil down. She felt like crying! She just couldn't figure out the word problem for math. Should she add? Multiply? Divide? The more she thought about it, the more confused she became. She didn't know what to do. Math was hard for her, but word problems were especially difficult.

After a few moments, Jennifer's eyes lit up and a smile broke out on her face. She nudged her friend, Julie. Julie was good at math. She would help her! "Julie, will you show me how to work this problem? I just can't figure out how to do it."

Julie smiled, "Sure, Jennifer, I'd be happy to."

A friend is always willing to share what he knows with you. A friend wants to help you understand things that are difficult for you to understand. If you are God's friend, He promises to share what He knows with you. He promises to help you understand. Because God is your friend He is always happy to give you the wisdom you need if you ask.

Hide and Seek Words ☐

As you read your Bible try to find these hidden words:

" . . . good success"

Be a Success

Rick wanted to be a success with his model car. His school's annual Model Contest would be tomorrow and he still had wheels to paint, along with the final coat and touch-ups. He was worried; would he have time to finish it?

All of a sudden, Rick heard his friend, Jeff, say "Hi! How's it coming? I'm so excited. It's almost as if it was my car and me entering the contest instead of you." Jeff laughed. But Rick wasn't laughing.

"Jeff, I'm really worried. I don't know if I'm going to have enough time to finish it. I still have a lot to do."

Jeff smiled, "Don't worry, Rick, I'll help you. I want you to do the best you can." Jeff's smile widened to a big grin. "I want you to be a real success." This time they both laughed.

Rick said, "Thanks, Jeff, you're a real friend."

God is your friend. He wants you to do your very best and be your very best. If you obey His Word, you have His promise to help you be a good success.

Hide and Seek Words ☐
As you read your Bible try to find these hidden words:

"Happy is he . . ."

I'd Be Happy If . . .

Have you ever said that to a friend? Did a friend ever say it to you? Let's see if you can fill in the end of the sentence. Say to yourself, "I'd be happy if _____ " and then say all the things you think would make you happy.

You might have said a new bike, or a television of your very own, or maybe $100. Those things might make you happy for a while, but what would happen when the bike got old, the television went on the blink and you spent your $100? You'd need something else to make you happy, wouldn't you?

God has a special happiness that He gives to His friends. His happiness never gets old, never wears out, and you can't use it up. God's happiness is given forever. It's the happiness you receive from just having Him as your friend. You become friends with God by receiving His Son, Jesus Christ. I'm happy because I have received Him as my Savior from sin. Is He your friend, too?

Hide and Seek Words ☐

As you read your Bible try to find these hidden words:

"Every good thing . . ."

What's a Good Thing?

Diane was puzzled. She asked her friend Gina, "What's a good thing, Gina?"

Gina thought for a moment. Then she said, "I'm not sure, Diane. I have a good home, good family and good friends like you. Those are good things to me."

Diane was still unsure, "What's a good thing to you, Jerry?"

"Pizza! French fries! Cokes! A good baseball mitt!" Jerry quickly answered.

Diane laughed, and then Jeff said, "A good thing to me is any good thing that happens to me during the week . . . or something that helps me or is good for me, I guess."

A grin began to form on Diane's face. "I think I understand now," she said. "Everything I need or that is good for me, whether it's family, friends, a home, clothes, food or experience is a good thing."

God says, every good thing given to you is from Him. God wants to give you good things because He is your friend.

Hide and Seek Words ☐

As you read your Bible try to find these hidden words:

" . . . my voice"

Caution! Danger Ahead!

Jamie rubbed his head as he leaned against his friend Keith. "I warned you, Jamie! You didn't hear me, but I warned you before about that bump at the end of the hill."

Still a bit shaky, Jamie answered, "I know I didn't hear you. Thanks for trying to protect me, Keith. You're a real friend."

A friend will warn you of danger because he doesn't want you to get hurt. You should warn your friends, too.

God wants to protect you from danger. He warns you in the Bible of many things that will hurt you. He also tells you what will be good for you and what will help you. Sometimes God warns you by speaking to your heart. If you are His friend you will know when God is warning you. You will know His voice.

Hide and Seek Words ☐
As you read your Bible try to find these hidden words:

"...through...comfort of the Scriptures...hope"

Need Some Encouragement?

"I don't think I can do it. I've tried and I just can't. I'll never be able to do it." Have you ever felt that way? Perhaps it was in a gym class. You were trying for several weeks to learn how to do a backbend. Maybe it was a math problem you just couldn't understand how to work. Then a friend said, "Sure, you can do it. Here, let me help you!"

A friend will encourage you when you are feeling down, or thinking that something is impossible. A friend will help you, encourage you, and give you hope.

God promises to encourage His friends. He

does it through the promises in the Scriptures. God has the power to give all that He promises to those He calls His friends. Next time you need a friend to encourage you, ask God!

Hide and Seek Words ☐

As you read your Bible try to find these hidden words:

"Thy thoughts . . . O God"

"I'm Thinking About You!"

Patti was excited! She didn't get mail very often. She quickly opened the envelope and pulled out a card. It was from her friend Julie in Arizona. The card read, "Just wanted to let you know I'm thinking about you." Patti spent a lot of time thinking about Julie. She was a special friend. Do you think about your friends? The things you like to do together and the fun you have?

The Bible says that God is thinking about you constantly. He thinks about you so much that you couldn't even count how many times He thinks

 of you. God thinks about you all the time! God is your friend. Friends think about each other. How often do you think about Him?

Hide and Seek Words ☐

As you read your Bible try to find these hidden words:

" . . . the God of hope"

Hope Instead of Wish!

What do you mean when you say you are hoping for something? Do you know what is means to hope? Do you know there is a difference between wishing and hoping? Here's an example. If you wish for a new bike for your birthday, you mean you want a new bike. If you hope for a new bike for your birthday, you mean you not only want a new bike, but you expect to get one. Hope is wanting something and then *believing* you will get it!

The Bible says that God gives you hope and keeps you happy and full of peace as you believe in Him. Psalm 146:5 says, "Happy is he . . . whose hope is in the Lord his God." If you

want the happiness and peace God promises to His friends, believe that God will give them to you and He will.

Hope in God!

Hide and Seek Words ☐

As you read your Bible try to find these hidden words:

"Greater love hath no man..."

Saving a Friend's Life!

Todd took long deep breaths...the air rushing into his lungs felt good. He never realized what a wonderful thing it was to breathe! He leaned over and looked at his friend Carl on the ground. Carl's chest was rising and falling at a steady pace now. His eyes opened, and he looked up at Todd. Todd smiled. It had been a close call.

Carl wasn't a very good swimmer and in the excitement of their first spring outing, he had ventured too far out into the lake. If Todd had not seen him when he did, Carl would have drowned. Todd was shaking. He hadn't realized till now how frightened he had been...for Carl and himself. He just knew he had to try to save his friend's life.

Jesus Christ has given His life for you so that you can live forever. He has shown you how much God wants to be your friend. "Greater love hath no man than this, that a man lay down his life for his friends" (John 15:13).

Hide and Seek Words ☐

As you read your Bible try to find these hidden words:

"...assembling...ourselves together"

Now That You're Friends!

Since Brady and Ben became friends they have been spending a lot of time together. The more they get to know each other, the more they like each other and want to be together. That's the way friends are!

When you become friends with God, He wants you to spend time with Him every day too! He wants you to get to know Him better by talking with Him in your prayers and by reading His Word. God wants you to know what He has promised you now that you are His friend. He tells you about Himself and His promises in the Bible.

Another way you can know God better is by being with other friends of His, "assemble together," talk about Him together, learn about the Lord Jesus by reading and studying the Bible and praying together. Sunday school is a wonderful place for God's friends to meet every week!

Hide and Seek Words □

As you read your Bible try to find these hidden words:

"If ye forgive"

I Forgive You!

Gym class had just been dismissed. It was time for recess. Jamie and Steve walked up to their teacher, "Miss Porter," Jamie said, "We have a problem. We had a fight in gym class."

Miss Porter asked, "Why were you fighting?" After listening to both of them, Miss Porter said, "There seems to have been a misunderstanding. What should you do about it?"

Jamie answered, "I think we should say we're sorry to each other." Steve agreed and apologies were exchanged.

Then Miss Porter asked, "Now...do you forgive one another?"

When a friend says, "I'm sorry," it's important to let him know that you won't hold a grudge. When you forgive a friend, you forget that he ever hurt you. That's what God has done for you. If you tell God you are sorry for your sins, God forgives you. He forgets your sin.

Just as God has forgiven you, God wants you to be able to say, "I forgive," to others. Will you do this for Him?

Hide and Seek Words ☐

As you read your Bible try to find these hidden words:

"Ye are my friends"

If You Obey

DANGEROUS CURVE AHEAD! FALL-ING ROCKS! SLIPPERY WHEN WET! Have you ever seen those signs along the road? They are warning signs to motorists. The purpose of the signs is to prevent accidents and keep people from getting hurt. Warning signs also protect people who aren't driving. SLOW DOWN! PEDESTRIAN CROSSWALK! SCHOOL CROSSING! are all signs that help protect people who are walking. Warning signs . . . if they are obeyed, help to protect people.

God wants to protect you from harm, too. He knows you need some warning signs as you travel along life's road. He has given you signs—commandments—to live by, so that you won't get hurt or hurt somebody else. A friend cares enough about you to protect you from harm. When you obey God's command-ments, you have His help and pro-tection. Not only that, you show you are His friend if you obey Him.

Hide and Seek Words ☐

As you read your Bible try to find these hidden words:

"Do ye . . . likewise"

Be Friendly!

Mrs. Abbot listed classroom jobs on the chalkboard as her class discussed what was needed in the room. Patti mentioned a need for book arrangers. Jean suggested someone should take care of the fish aquarium. Several other children added art helpers and bulletin board helpers.

Then Cheryl suggested a need for a classroom host or hostess. The other children agreed. Someone was needed to make visitors feel welcome and comfortable in their classroom. The students began to discuss what makes a good host or hostess: "Someone who says 'Hi!' to people"; "Someone who smiles"; "Someone who takes time to show people around the room"; "Someone who listens to and answers questions." The class decided that what was needed was someone who was truly friendly!

God wants you to be friendly. When you are friendly to someone, you show you are a friend of God.

Hide and Seek Words ☐

As you read your Bible try to find these hidden words:

"Commit thy way unto the Lord"

Better Than Ever!

Ann looked out the window. A smile crossed over her face. She had been looking forward to today. It seemed like spring would never come, and here it was...at last!

Ann kept thinking, "*Today! Today! Today!*" She had been patiently waiting all winter for the park's recreation program to start, and today was the day! Ann had been planning to go to the arts and crafts class. She wanted to make oodles of things! She had even told her friend Betsy about it. She was secretly hoping that Betsy would be able to go to the classes with her. Ann knew if Betsy was there, she would have an even better time!

When you are God's friend, He wants you to share your plans with Him. He wants to be a part of all you do. When you trust Him with your plans, He will help you work them out in the best way possible. He promises to make your plans better than ever!

Hide and Seek Words ☐

As you read your Bible try to find these hidden words:

"Thanks be unto God . . ."

Have You Thanked Him?

"Jimmy, someone's at the door. Will you see who it is?"

Jimmy looked out the window and saw his best friend, Tom, standing at the door. He had something in his hands. "It's Tom." Jimmy was happy to see his buddy. As he opened the door, he could see a big grin on Tom's face.

"Hi, Jimmy," Tom said, "I've brought you something . . . it's a gift from me to you. I know it's not your birthday or anything like that. I just wanted you to know I'm glad you're my friend."

Tom held out the gift to Jimmy. Jimmy stood speechless. He didn't know what to say. Finally, he was able to say, "Thanks, Tom. I really don't deserve this. You've been a better friend to me than I've been to you . . . but thanks. Thanks a lot!

God is your friend. He has given you the most important gift He could ever give . . . His Son, Jesus Christ! Have you accepted Him? When you accept Jesus Christ as your friend, you have accepted God's gift to you. Have you thanked Him for His gift?

Talking with God

Hide and Seek Words ☐

As you read your Bible try to find these hidden words:

"The Lord will hear"

Call on God

David was a man who loved God very much. He sang and talked to God. David knew that *God* would hear and help him. God told him to write down his songs and prayers. They are called psalms and are now part of God's book, the Bible.

God wants *you* to talk to Him, too. When you call (pray), God will hear you.

Prayer is not only talking to God but *listening* to Him. God does not say words out loud. He speaks to your heart. God speaks when you read your Bible. You can talk to God often.

Share your questions, problems and joys with Him.

God promises in the Bible that He will hear you and answer when you call to Him.

Hide and Seek Words ☐
As you read your Bible try to find these hidden words:

"Commune with your own heart upon your bed"

Sin Separates from God

David, the psalm writer, knew that sin separates us from God because God is holy.

In Romans 3:23 we read, "For all have sinned and come short of the glory of God."

Every person has sinned. That is why God sent His Son, Jesus, into the world. When Jesus died on the cross He took on Himself your sins and the sins of all the people of the world.

If you believe Jesus died for your sins, ask Him to forgive you. He will. God hears you when you talk to Him. Every night when you go to bed, you can think about God. Like David you can talk to God and be God's friend.

Hide and Seek Words ☐

As you read your Bible try to find these hidden words:

"Thou . . . art become my salvation"

A Gift from God

The psalmist, David, knew that salvation was a gift from God. He thanked God for his salvation.

Mindy's Sunday school teacher told her that Jesus died on the cross for her sins. Over and over the teacher told Mindy how to be saved—by believing Jesus died for her and receiving Him into her heart. Mindy prayed for forgiveness but she still did not think she was saved.

Then the teacher gave Mindy a Bible as a gift.

Mindy took it and said, "Thank you."

"Mindy," her taecher said, "why don't you just say 'thank You' to Jesus for His gift of salvation?"

Finally, Mindy understood. Salvation is a gift from God!

If you ask Jesus to forgive your sins and ask Him to give you the gift of salvation, He will. Just take it by believing it is yours. Don't forget to say "thank You"!

Hide and Seek Words ☐

As you read your Bible try to find these hidden words:

**"His [God's] praise shall
continually be in my mouth"**

Friends Talk to Each Other a Lot

If you believe on Jesus you are a child of God. Your Heavenly Father is your friend.

Jim and Eddie are friends. They sit together at lunch. They play together at recess. They walk home from school together. Jim and Eddie talk to each other a lot.

Friends spend time together. Friends talk to each other a lot. David was God's friend. David talked to God while he watched the sheep. He praised God often. He spent time with God.

You need to talk to God, too. The Bible says, "Pray without ceasing" (1 Thessalonians 5:17). To pray without ceasing means to pray every

day. How long has it been since you talked to God?

God wants you to spend time talking to Him. Tell God that you love Him. Tell Him how much you enjoy the good things that He gives you . . . right now!

Hide and Seek Words ☐

As you read your Bible try to find these hidden words:

"Evening and morning, and at noon, will I pray"

When Should You Talk to God?

The psalmist said he prayed to the Lord every day. He prayed when he was sad. He prayed when he was happy. He asked God for help. He thanked God for things. He praised God.

You can talk to God whenever you think of God. You can pray every day or you can pray every hour. Talk to God often.

I talk to God in the morning.
I talk to God at night.
I talk to God in-between times,
To keep things going right.
I tell God every problem.

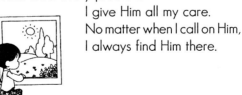

I give Him all my care.
No matter when I call on Him,
I always find Him there.

Hide and Seek Words ☐

As you read your Bible try to find these hidden words:

"Whither shall I flee from thy presence?"

Where Is God?

There is a story about a man who wanted to find God. He walked the streets of the city and hunted for God but he didn't find God. He walked out to the country. He still didn't find God. Then, he decided to climb a high hill and see if God was there. At the end of the day, the man was tired. He sat down. He finally got quiet. He started to read his Bible. He discovered that God was with him all the time.

Where does the Bible say God is?

God is everywhere. He is behind you. He is

in front of you. He is with you. If you are a Christian, God is in you. There isn't any place that God cannot go. You can talk to God anywhere, because God is everywhere.

Hide and Seek Words ☐

As you read your Bible try to find these hidden words:

"O Lord . . . I cry unto thee"

Brian Prayed Under Water

Brian was wading in the creek. Suddenly, he seemed to step out into nothing and the water was over his head. Brian felt himself coming up and then going down again. He held his breath and fought the water. Brian couldn't swim.

"Please, God, don't let me die!" Brian prayed while he was under water.

Just then Steve saw Brian come up in the water. Steve went swimming toward Brian. It was hard work. Steve managed to float Brian to the bank and pull him to safety.

Ask Brian if you have to be on your knees when you pray. Ask Brian if you can only pray before you go to bed. He'll tell you that you can talk to God any time—anywhere!

Hide and Seek Words ☐
As you read your Bible try to find these hidden words:

" . . . teach me thy paths"

God's Way

The Bible says David, who wrote many of the Psalms, was a man after God's own heart. David loved God. He wanted to please Him.

David asked God to teach him what to do and say. When David had to make a decision, he talked to God about it. He asked God to show him the right way to live.

There are times when you must decide what to do. You can ask God to help you make decisions.

Before you read the Bible ask God to help you understand what you read. Like David you can pray, "Show me thy ways, O Lord."

God wants you to ask Him to teach you His way.

Hide and Seek Words ☐

As you read your Bible try to find these hidden words:

"I will guide thee"

God Will Guide You

David knew about danger and he prayed to God for help. Several times David had to hide from King Saul who wanted to kill him. Saul hated David and hunted him but God helped David hide. God told David what to do.

Walter was a prisoner during World War II. God helped him escape from prison even though there were lots of prison guards around. Before Walter made his escape he prayed, "Lord, what shall I do?" Every time he was in danger he prayed. God led him to safety.

God wants to teach and guide all of His children. God wants to guide you!

Hide and Seek Words ☐

As you read your Bible try to find these hidden words:

"...they cried unto the Lord in their trouble"

Ask for Help

David, the psalmist, found that God helped him when he had a problem. God still helps people today.

Dawn outgrew her new school clothes. She was so tall that her clothes were all too short. Dawn's parents did not have the money to buy new clothes for her.

"If it is that important to you, why don't you pray about it?" Dawn's mother suggested. "God will help you with your troubles."

Dawn did talk to God about her clothes. A few days later, she was given some new clothes that fit her perfectly! Dawn knew it was God who answered her prayer!

When you have a problem, you can talk to God about it. The Lord will help you too.

Hide and Seek Words ☐

As you read your Bible try to find these hidden words:

"I will deliver thee"

Police Catch a Prowler

Roger was sure he heard a prowler outside the house. His parents were gone and he was all alone!

Roger went to the phone. On the wall his mother had placed a card with the phone number of the police. Roger dialed the number.

The police station was not far away. A policeman answered the phone and sent the patrol car to Roger's house. Soon the police caught the prowler. Roger was safe!

God is something like a policeman. When you call He is always ready to answer you. You can talk to God when you have troubles. God will take care of you.

Hide and Seek Words □

As you read your Bible try to find these hidden words:

**" . . . he bringeth them out
of their distresses"**

The Storm Comes

David, the psalmist, told about a storm at sea. People on a ship did not know what to do. They prayed to God. David told how God helped them. God is in control.

Shelly loved to spend the night with her aunt but when a thunderstorm came up the room seemed strange. Shelly was afraid.

There was a flash of lightning—a crash of thunder! The street light outside the window went out. The room was dark.

Shelly's aunt came into the room with a candle. She sat down on the bed beside Shelly.

Shelly and her aunt talked about times when God had taken care of them. Shelly was not afraid anymore. She was thinking about how God was with them even when there was a storm.

Hide and Seek Words ☐

As you read your Bible try to find these hidden words:

"I will be with him in trouble"

Tell God About It

All through the Psalms David tells how God helped him. When David had a problem, he prayed about it. David said, "God is our refuge and strength, a very present help in time of trouble" (Psalm 46:1).

Megan and Lindsay were sad. Their daddy was an alcoholic. He left home. Then mother was sad, too.

Lindsay wanted her daddy to be with them. She talked to God about it. She asked God to help her daddy quit drinking and come home. After she talked to God she felt better.

After many days had passed Lindsay's daddy did come home. God had helped her daddy quit drinking. The family was happy. They all went to church together. They said, "Thank You, God."

When you talk to God about your troubles, you will feel better, too. Tell God about your problems. God has promised to help!

Hide and Seek Words ☐
As you read your Bible try to find these hidden words:

"... saved him out of all his troubles"

Mitch Needed Money!

Mitch's dad was a carpenter and couldn't work in rainy weather. After many rainy days there was no food in the house. Mitch went out to play by the stadium, trying to forget he was hungry. Finally he prayed for money to buy food. A thought came to him, *I'll look under the bleachers in the stadium. Maybe I'll find some change.* Sure enough he found about three dollars altogether and took it home to his parents! They bought bread and milk right away. Mitch is grown now but he still remembers that day. He says, "God answered my prayer and helped me find the money."

God helps people who have troubles if they trust Him. If you need help, you can talk to God about it.

Hide and Seek Words ☐

As you read your Bible try to find these hidden words:

"I love the Lord, because he hath heard my voice"

Ask God to Help

Sandra had a problem. Although she was nine years old, Sandra still wet the bed at night. Sandra was going to visit her aunt for a whole week. She was worried for she knew she was too big to wet the bed.

The first evening at her aunt's house, Sandra was reading the Bible with her aunt. They read, "If ye shall ask anything in my name, I will do it" (John 14:14).

Sandra told her aunt, "I am going to ask God to help me not to wet the bed tonight."

The next morning Sandra found that she had not wet the bed! Sandra smiled. "Thank You, God," she said.

God helped Sandra all week.

When you have a problem, you can talk to God about it. God will hear and help you.

Hide and Seek Words ☐

As you read your Bible try to find these hidden words:

"My meditation of him shall be sweet"

Thinking About God

Do you know what it means to meditate? When you meditate you spend time thinking about God. David took time to meditate. The Psalms are filled with David's thoughts about God.

David liked to play the harp. Sometimes, when he thought about God, he would sing about the things God had done.

After you read your Bible, you can think about God. You may want to sing a song, too. You may even want to memorize a special verse of the Bible. Write the verse that you think about today on the lines below.

_____

_____

_____

_____

Hide and Seek Words ☐

As you read your Bible try to find these hidden words:

"I will be glad . . . I will sing . . ."

Sing to the Lord

Singing is a way of talking to God. Many songs praise God. Here is a song for you to sing. Can you play this song on an instrument?

Sing to The Lord

L. Flanagan

Sing to the Lord who loves you

Sing to the Lord who cares.

Sing to the Lord who saves you

And answers all your prayers:

Hide and Seek Words ☐

As you read your Bible try to find these hidden words:

"Be still and know that I am God"

Marsha Listens

Marsha was sitting under a big tree. She looked sad.

"Why aren't you playing?" Marsha's mother asked.

"I am listening for God's voice but I can't hear Him. Mr. Baker said in church that he has heard God speak many times. Why can't I hear God?" Marsha asked.

"God speaks in many ways," Marsha's mother told her. "God speaks to us by His beautiful creation. God speaks through your teachers and parents. Most of all God talks to you through the Bible. Read your Bible. Then be still and think about what you have read. God will speak to your heart."

When you talk to God, remember to be still and listen. He will put His thoughts in your mind and heart.

Hide and Seek Words ☐

As you read your Bible try to find these hidden words:

" . . . **the meditation of my heart**"

Thinking About God's Word

Shelly and Trudi were best friends. One day Trudi got mad and would not play with Shelly. When Shelly tried to find out what was wrong, Trudi went to play with Jane.

That night Shelly read in the Bible about Stephen who was stoned because he believed on Jesus. As Stephen was dying he prayed for those who hated him, "Lord, lay not this sin to their charge..." (Acts 7:60).

Shelly thought (meditated) about what she had read for a long time. She knew she needed to forgive Trudi. Then she prayed for her. God helped Shelly forgive.

God wants you to meditate (think) about what you read in His Word, then try to do what it tells you. Talk to God about what you will do and ask for His help.

Hide and Seek Words □

As you read your Bible try to find these hidden words:

" . . . thy thoughts which are to us-ward"

God Thinks About You

In Psalm 40, David is saying that God thinks about YOU.

God sees, hears and cares about each one of His children, but it is also true that the Bible is full of God's thoughts and promises. The Bible is like a letter from God—written to you!

As you read the Bible, look for promises of what God wants to do for you and believe Him! In Psalm 139 David tells that God's thoughts about us are so many we can't even count them!

God is thinking about you. Do you think about Him?

Hide and Seek Words ☐

As you read your Bible try to find these hidden words:

" . . . **worship the Lord**"

What Is Worship?

Worship is more than saying words. It is a way of thinking about God in your heart.

When you say, "Thank You, God," you are thinking about what He has done for you. When you worship God you are thinking about who He is and what He does.

Think with me for a few minutes....

God is the Creator of everything that is good and beautiful. God is powerful and holy. God knows everything.

God is love. God loves you and wants you to love Him back. Tell God that you love Him.

You can worship God anytime and anywhere. To help you think of God, read one of the Psalms. Then, talk to God like David did. Tell God how wonderful you think He is!

Hide and Seek Words ☐

As you read your Bible try to find these hidden words:

"O come let us worship"

Why Go to Church?

Have you ever heard a grown-up say, "I can worship God at the lake just as well as I can at church"?

You can talk to God and feel Him near when you sit on a bank with a fishing pole in your hand, but you also need to attend church. You need to get together with other Christians to sing and pray. At church you can learn more about God.

Without eating lots of good food with vitamins and minerals in it you will not grow big and strong. You need spiritual food—God's Word—too. At church you will receive spiritual food which will help you grow to be a healthy child of God.

You can worship God anywhere but you also need to go to church, God's house. Hebrews 10:25 says that's important!

Hide and Seek Words ☐
As you read your Bible try to find these hidden words:

"Every day will I bless thee"

When to Praise

When you are in trouble, you remember to pray. You ask God for help. However, it is not enough to pray or praise God only when you are in trouble.

In James 5:13 the Bible says to sing Psalms when you are merry or happy.

God wants you to talk to Him when you feel good. He wants to share your happy times too!

God is interested in you no matter how you feel. If you are unhappy, talking to God can make you feel better. If you are happy, thank God for the things that make you feel happy.

God deserves your praise. David, the man who wrote many of the Psalms, knew that God wants our praise. Like David, you should bless God by praising Him every day.

Hide and Seek Words ☐

As you read your Bible try to find these hidden words:

" . . . **filled with thy praise**"

God Is Great!

A farm boy who went away to college sent a Mother's Day card home. On the envelope he had written: "To the greatest mom in the world."

Many Mother's Day or Father's Day cards say "the greatest." We praise our parents by telling them that we love, admire or honor them.

To praise God is to tell Him how much He means to us. God is truly the greatest. We are grateful for all the things He has done for us. The Bible says, "We love him, because he first loved us" (1 John 4:19).

Next time you talk to God why not tell Him how much you love Him? Let God know that you think He is the greatest.

Hide and Seek Words ☐

As you read your Bible try to find these hidden words:

"I am fearfully and wonderfully made"

Helping Hands

David believed God had created him. But David probably did not know as much about the body as you do, because you have studied about the body in school.

David used his hands every day. He knew how wonderful it is to have hands that can do things.

David knew he could fold his hands and talk to God.

David knew he could reach out his hands to help someone else.

Can you name some things you can do with your hands?

God wants human hands to do His work. He can use your hands. Will you let Him?

Maybe you could help a smaller brother or sister. Your hands might help your parents or friends and neighbors. Praise God for the hands He gave you.

Hide and Seek Words ☐
As you read your Bible try to find these hidden words:

" . . . praise the name of the Lord"

Praise Him for All Things

Tonight—look out your window. If it isn't cloudy you can see stars that are billions of miles away. Our own sun (a star) is said to be 93 million miles away!

Can you find a planet? The earth (a planet) is really a remarkable creation. If the earth was any closer to the sun you would be too hot. If the earth was any farther from the sun you would freeze. God planned our planet just right for you to live on.

The more you study science and the more you learn about the wonderful world and universe, the more reason you have to praise God.

David wrote Psalm 148 to praise God whose hand created all things. Read this Psalm and then praise God!

Hide and Seek Words ☐
As you read your Bible try to find these hidden words:
"I will offer to thee . . . thanksgiving"

The Birthday Party

Don went to Martin's birthday party. Martin got many presents. He opened them as fast as he could and did not say thank you to anyone. When Martin's gifts were all opened, he screamed, "Is that all I get?" He got mad and started yelling, "I want a pony."

Martin's mother said, "The party is over."

Don went home. He felt sad. He had spent all his week's allowance to buy Martin's gift and Martin did not even like it. Martin did not thank Don for the gift.

When you talk to God are you like Martin? Do you say, "Give me," all the time? Are you always asking God for things? Do you ever stop to say, "Thank You, God"? It pleases God to know you like His gifts to you.

Hide and Seek Words □

As you read your Bible try to find these hidden words:

"O give thanks unto the Lord"

Thank You, God

"Before I was married," Aunt Brenda said, "I lived alone in a mobile home. Late one night I heard a noise outside. I was afraid. It sounded like someone trying to break in! I did not have a phone or any weapons. The nearest neighbor was gone. I asked God to protect me. Then, I heard the neighbor's big dog barking and footsteps running away. I went to sleep. I know that God was watching over me. The next morning, I found the door unlocked and foot-prints in the snow. I said, 'Thank You, God, for taking care of me.' "

David talked to God often and he always thanked God when He helped him.

Can you think of times that God has pro-tected you—playing? At school? Traveling? Thank Him right now!

Hide and Seek Words ☐

As you read your Bible try to find these hidden words:

"... be thankful unto him"

Bump Is Grateful

Ron had a little black dog named Country Bumpkin. "Bump" is a good dog but he cannot do much for himself. Ron has to feed and give water to Bump every day.

Bump wags his tail when Ron takes care of him. Sometimes Bump licks Ron's hand. When Ron sits in his chair, Bump climbs up beside him. Bump follows Ron around and loves Ron because he is grateful for all Ron does for him.

A dog, just an animal, is sometimes more grateful to his master than we are to God. Yet, God has given us *everything* that we have!

Are you grateful? What are some things that you can thank God for today?

_____

_____

_____

Hide and Seek Words ☐

As you read your Bible try to find these hidden words:

"I will praise thee, O Lord"

Praise the Lord!

The whole book of Psalms is filled with praise to God. David talked about God a lot. He praised God because He made:

the land and seas,
the wind, the sky,
the grass, the trees,
and birds that fly.

David praised God because He is:

"...full of compassion,
and gracious,
longsuffering,
and plenteous in mercy and truth" (Psalm 86:15).

Make a list of reasons you praise God.

_____

_____

_____

Wisdom from God

Hide and Seek Words ☐

As you read your Bible try to find these hidden words:

"The fear of the Lord is the beginning of knowledge"

Knowledge Is from Above

Proverbs is a book of knowledge and wisdom. But you cannot really understand the book of Proverbs until you know and fear God.

Fearing God means to respect Him reverently—to let Him take charge of your life.

Samuel was only a boy when God spoke to him one night. Samuel answered, "Speak; for your servant hears" (1 Samuel 3:10). God was so pleased with Samuel's obedience that He caused others to listen when Samuel spoke (see

1 Samuel 3:19). People must have thought Samuel was very smart indeed.

Do you want your words to be wise? Like Samuel, you must listen as God speaks to you through the Bible. Respect and obey God and He will teach you many things.

Hide and Seek Words ☐

As you read your Bible try to find these hidden words:

"My son, hear
the instruction of thy father"

Happiness in Obedience

Tom's parents gave him a puppy. Every day he went to the garage to feed it.

One day as he went, Father said, "Tom, be sure the door latches when you leave!"

An hour later, while playing with his furry puppy, Tom heard his sister call, "Tom-e-e-e, your TV program's started!" Tom dropped the pup and gave the door a tug as he ran for the house.

Next morning Father woke Tom and told him some sad news. The puppy had pushed the unlatched garage door open and could not be found!

God gives us rules to help us, just as Tom's father told him to be sure and latch the garage door. One of these rules is "Learn [or obey] the instructions of your father." Did Tom obey?

Hide and Seek Words □

As you read your Bible try to find these hidden words:

"If sinners entice [tempt] thee, consent thou not"

Do Friends Tempt Us?

You have probably heard how Satan tempted Eve. He spoke through a beautiful serpent and got Eve to disobey God (see Genesis 3:1-6).

Perhaps you think that temptation comes only from Satan, but God's Word says, "all have sinned" (Romans 3:23). Not one person can say he is not a sinner—not you nor I. Because of this, even good friends sometimes tempt each other to do wrong.

Anne had permission to play at Mary's house until five o'clock. At five Mary's favorite TV program came on. "Will you stay and watch this program with me?" Mary asked.

"Mother said I must come home at five," replied Anne.

Mary coaxed, "It's only half an hour. Your mother won't notice if you stay a few more minutes."

Anne remembered Proverbs 1:10, "If sinners entice thee . . ." What should she do?

Hide and Seek Words ☐

As you read your Bible try to find these hidden words:

"The Lord giveth wisdom"

How to Really Be Wise

You may think that only old men who think a lot are wise. But God wants *you* to be wise.

Have you ever worried about a tough decision, such as what to buy a friend for his birthday? You may have asked someone for an idea, and they said, "Can't you make up your own mind?" You know some things you can get, but you can't decide what your friend would like best. Knowledge is only facts—what you have learned—stored in your head. Wisdom is the ability to make good decisions. If you need wisdom, ask God. He will give it without scolding (see James 1:5).

God, who wisely gave His Son to die for you, wants you to be wise. The wisest thing you can do is to receive the Lord Jesus as your Savior from sin.

Hide and Seek Words ☐

As you read your Bible try to find these hidden words:

"The upright shall dwell in the land . . . but the wicked shall be cut off [separated]"

Honesty Pays

An upright person is honest. He does not lie, steal or cheat.

Ed didn't like school. He cheated to try to get even with his parents for sending him to school. Soon his teachers didn't want him and the principal suspended him. He began to play with rough boys who stole. Ed was arrested and put in jail for shoplifting. He was separated from his parents because of his wickedness.

Today, although Ed doesn't steal, he is often "cut off" [separated] from good jobs because people don't like to hire a person who's been in jail.

God gives each person a place in life where he can be happy and satisfied. If you are wicked and dishonest, this good place in life will be taken away and you will be miserable.

Hide and Seek Words ☐
As you read your Bible try to find these hidden words:

"Let not mercy . . . forsake thee"

Mercy In a Pencil?

Some people hurt others to show people they are tough. But God tells *you* to be kind. Mercy is being kind to people even though you may think they don't deserve it!

Suppose someone comes to class without a pencil. Perhaps he has been mean to you. You may think, *If he's dumb enough to forget his pencil, he can borrow one from the teacher.* But then you think, *Would I want the teacher to scold me for forgetting my pencil?* You can show mercy by offering him your extra pencil.

You have sinned and do not deserve God's favor but God showed you mercy by sending His Son Jesus to die for your sins. Have you believed on the Lord Jesus Christ? If not, do so today.

Hide and Seek Words ☐
As you read your Bible try to find these hidden words:

"Trust in the Lord"

Not Ashamed!

Tom and his dad were walking through the forest. They came to a log bridge. Dad started across first. "Come on, Tom," he said, "let me take your hand."

"I can cross alone," said Tom stubbornly, so Dad went on ahead. Tom got down on his hands and knees to crawl.

Patiently, Dad waited as Tom crawled to the middle, then stopped and called out, "Help me!" With his hand in Dad's, Tom crossed safely.

You may be like Tom. Perhaps you are ashamed to admit you need God's help. But the Bible says, "Whoever believes on him [Jesus] shall not be ashamed" (Romans 10:11). Will you trust Jesus today?

Hide and Seek Words □

As you read your Bible try to find these hidden words:

"In all thy ways acknowledge him, and he shall direct thy paths"

Remember God

Many years ago a group of men met to plan our country's government. The meeting lasted for several days, but they could only argue.

One day a wise and famous man, Benjamin Franklin, told the men, "I suggest we start each day with prayer."

So daily the men prayed and asked God's help before they began their meeting. Because they acknowledged God (remembered God's importance) the government these men planned gave Americans more freedom than any other nation.

The government plans made long ago in Philadelphia are called the *Constitution of the United States.*

The Bible reminds you to remember God "in all your ways." If you do this, God will show you the best plans for your life.

Hide and Seek Words ☐

As you read your Bible try to find these hidden words:

"Be not wise in thine own eyes"

Unwise Tom

Tom had worked for Mrs. Jones for three Saturdays. She had shown him how to carefully trim around her flowers with the power mower.

Today Tom was in a hurry; ball practice began at two o'clock. *What does Mrs. Jones know about mowing lawns,* he thought to himself as he buzzed along, pushing the new mower between some stones which bordered the flowers.

WHAM! THUMP! THUMP! THUMP! The mower shook violently as Tom quickly shut it off. "What's the matter, Tom?" Mrs. Jones asked, as he bent over the mower. There was no hiding the damage. Oil gushed from the broken mower engine!

Tom walked home sadder and wiser. He had no job, and not enough money for his uniform which he must have to play in the baseball league. How he wished he had remembered Proverbs 3:7. He had thought he was wiser than Mrs. Jones. Was he?

Hide and Seek Words ☐
As you read your Bible try to find these hidden words:

"Honor the Lord with . . . the firstfruits"

We Give And God Gives

Some of the best parts of God's Word are the instructions with happy promises.

Today's verse tells you to give the Lord your "firstfruits." From all that you receive, you are to first give something to God. God's promise to you for "honoring" Him with the "first" part of your earnings or allowance is "plenty" (see Proverbs 3:10).

Do you often think your allowance isn't enough? Do you some- times find yourself bor- rowing money? Try this. From every dollar you receive, put aside ten cents for God. Put it in the Sunday school or church offering. Ask God to help you wisely use the money you have left. You will have "plenty" for the things you need.

Hide and Seek Words ☐

As you read your Bible try to find these hidden words:

"Whom the Lord loveth he correcteth"

One Reason for Parents

Anne was angry! All afternoon Mother had been saying, "Anne, do this...Anne, do that." Anne sulked and argued. Soon her mother was cross, too.

Dad arrived home at five o'clock. He hung up his coat and listened. "Mother, you get on my nerves," Anne said loudly.

Soon, Anne's father was sitting with her on her bed. She was crying, for she had just been punished.

With his arm around her, Dad talked softly, "Anne, honey, years ago I was fired from my job because I argued with the boss. How much easier it would have been if my parents had loved me enough to correct me."

That evening, as Anne cheerfully helped with the dishes she had forgotten her punishment but she remembered that her parents loved her. Anne and her mother sang, "What a Friend We Have in Jesus," as they worked together.

Hide and Seek Words ☐

As you read your Bible try to find these hidden words:

"She [wisdom] is more precious than rubies"

Is Wisdom Wealth?

King Solomon was the richest king that Israel ever had. He was also the wisest man of his time.

Do you know that wisdom will bring you more happiness than great riches? Solomon

was wise, so he asked God for more wisdom. Even though he was rich, and knew that money bought fine things, he didn't ask for more money (1 Kings 3:7-13). He knew that wisdom was more important than money.

Today wickedness is everywhere. Rioting and fighting are going on somewhere in the world almost all the time.

Trouble is caused because people are wicked. But much trouble comes also because people are unwise. Wisdom could prevent wars and save lives. Do you want to honor God? Like Solomon, ask God for wisdom. (See James 1:5.)

Hide and Seek Words ☐

As you read your Bible try to find these hidden words:

" . . . thou shalt not be afraid"

Night Safety

Tom shared a room with his younger brother, Bill. One night Bill awoke, crying. He had a bad dream and was afraid. Bill cried until Tom trudged upstairs to waken his parents.

"What's the matter, Bill?" asked Dad as he comforted him.

"I'm afraid to be alone. Can't I sleep with you?" Bill wailed.

"No, Bill." Dad hugged him close and prayed, "Dear Father, You loved us enough to send Your Son, Jesus, to die for our sins. Watch over Bill tonight and take his fear away."

Then Bill prayed, "Heavenly Father, I know You love me and will keep me safe tonight."

Tom and Bill remembered God's promise, "When you lie down, you shall not be afraid." Both boys slept soundly the rest of the night.

Hide and Seek Words ☐

As you read your Bible try to find these hidden words:

**"Withhold not good . . .
to whom it is due"**

Doing Good to Grandmother

Tom's grandmother always sent him gifts. For his birthday she had given him a fine watch which switched from time to date when he pressed a button.

Mother was writing a letter as Tom came home from school one day. "Do you want to add something to my letter to Grandmother, Tom?" she asked pleasantly.

"Naw," answered Tom, as he began to leave. Then he thought of the watch he was wearing. Grandmother had been good to him, and he loved her, too.

"Mother, I'll write to Grandmother," Tom said. "I know it will make her very glad if I say 'thank you' for my new watch."

You should be good to everyone. But God has given you special people to whom you can do good in a way no one else can. Can you think of someone to whom you should do good today?

Hide and Seek Words ☐

As you read your Bible try to find these hidden words:

" . . . the prosperity [riches] of fools shall destroy them"

A Rich Monkey

To trap monkeys in Africa, a gourd with bait inside is placed in the forest. A hole is cut in the gourd just large enough for the monkey to put in his paw. But the hole is too small to pull the paw out with a fistful of bait. The greedy monkey will not let go of the bait and so he is caught!

Proverbs 1:32 means that a fool is a person who trusts his riches—who would rather have money than God.

God has riches more important than money

and success. These riches are not gotten by being greedy. God's riches are a gift (Romans 6:23)! You can have His gift of eternal life by trusting Jesus as your Savior.

Hide and Seek Words ☐

As you read your Bible try to find these hidden words:

"Let thine eyes look right on"

Watch What You See!

Tom stopped by some boys on the sidewalk. They stood in front of a theater looking at a poster, laughing and joking. Tom knew some of the boys in the group.

As he passed, a boy yelled, "Hey, Tom, look here!" What Tom saw filled him with shame. People were killing and doing other wicked things. He walked quickly away.

That evening Tom read in his Bible. "Whatever things are honest... just... pure... lovely... of good report...think on these things" (Philippians 4:8).

The things that you look at are probably what you will think about. Many things in the world are ugly and wicked. Many things are also private and personal and should not be looked at to laugh about. The Bible tells us to think about pure and lovely things.

Often our eyes must look straight ahead. Tom wisely obeyed God's Word when he left the crowd and went home.

Hide and Seek Words ☐

As you read your Bible try to find these hidden words:

" . . . the eyes of the Lord"

God Sees

Tom and Jeff were walking home from school. They walked through an alley along some fenced yards. "Come on, Tom," Jeff said, as they passed an unhitched gate. "Let's cut through here. Nobody's home."

"My dad said to stay out of people's yards," replied Tom.

"Who's to know?" Jeff asked.

"God knows," said Tom, as he walked away.

That evening Tom read Proverbs 5:21 in his Bible. *Does God really have eyes that see me?* he thought to himself. Tom felt good about leaving Jeff and not going through that yard. Probably they wouldn't have hurt anything. But they would have been trespassing.

Tom was growing in the Lord. He was learning that God expects obedience even when we may not understand why. Do you know God can see you even when your parents cannot? (See Psalm 139:7 and 12.) Do you obey God?

Hide and Seek Words ☐

As you read your Bible try to find these hidden words:

"Go to the ant thou sluggard [lazy person]"

Hard Work Equals Success

Tom pedaled home with his newspaper bag over his shoulder. He stopped beside the garage and slammed his bike against the wall.

"What's the matter?" his father asked as Tom slouched into the house. "I just saw Jeff with a new bike!" he explained. "My old bike is in bad shape. I need a good bike for this job!"

"Tell you what, Tom, I'll give you $40 toward any bike you want. You pay the rest," his father said.

The next day Tom visited a bicycle shop. The bike he wanted cost a lot more than $40! With it he could increase his paper route.

Tom thought, *If I saved most of my profits, after giving part to the Lord, I could have a lightweight bike in two or three months. But I could have a cheaper bike Friday when Dad gets paid!*

What do you think he should do?

Hide and Seek Words ☐

As you read your Bible try to find these hidden words:

" . . . six things doth the Lord hate"

Does God Hate?

You may have read that "God is love" (1 John 4:8). But did you know that God also hates?

God loves people, but He hates their wicked deeds. He hates six things, and the seventh thing He hates especially. These are:

1. pride
2. lying
3. murder
4. wicked thoughts
5. mischief
6. false witness

The seventh thing that God hates is *stirring up trouble among our brothers.* These may be brothers (or sisters) in our family, or other Christians. God may hate this sin more than the others, because troubles grow from fights.

You cannot claim to love God unless you show love to others. (See 1 John 4:20.)

Hide and Seek Words ☐

As you read your Bible try to find these hidden words:

"...the fear of the Lord is to hate evil"

What You Should Hate

Proverbs 8:13 puzzled Tom. *God hates evil, sure. But how can I hate evil?* Tom wondered.

One day Tom was walking with Jeff. They saw a man who seemed to be sick. His clothes were shabby, and he looked dirty. He staggered as he walked.

Jeff began to make fun of the man and laugh.

By and by the man sat down took out a bottle and drank, then tossed the bottle on the ground and walked away.

That evening Tom told his parents what he had seen and how Jeff behaved. "Son," said his father, "That poor man was drunk. He is sick—sick with sin which only Christ can cure."

That night Tom thought about what his dad had said, and about the poor, lonely man. Tom hated drunkenness. He now knew what it meant to hate evil.

Hide and Seek Words ☐

As you read your Bible try to find these hidden words:

"A wise son maketh a glad father"

Wise or Foolish?

Tom whizzed down the street on his new lightweight bike, throwing papers as he went. Since getting his new bike his paper route had more than doubled. By summer he would have enough money for a trip to camp.

As Tom pedaled along, he saw Jeff on his doorstep looking sad. "What's the matter, Jeff?" he asked.

"My bike's broken," Jeff answered.

Tom rememberd that Jeff had had a nice new bike. But he had noticed that it was getting rusty and bent. "What happened?" Tom asked.

"My dad backed the car over it," Jeff replied.

Tom didn't have to ask how that happened. He had heard Jeff's dad scolding him for leaving his bike in the driveway.

When Tom's dad got home that evening, he was pleased to find Tom's bike chained to a pipe in the garage. Father patted him on the back, "You are a very wise son, Tom."

Hide and Seek Words ☐

As you read your Bible try to find these hidden words:

"The lips of the righteous feed many"

Be a Good Shepherd

Anne knew that Psalm 23 was about a shepherd who led his sheep. Jesus is the shepherd and those who follow Him are His sheep. So, using her mother's reference Bible, she tried to discover as many places in the Bible as she could which talked about shepherds and sheep.

In 1 Peter 5:1 and 2, Anne learned that pastors, too, are like shepherds. They are supposed to feed God's people, His sheep. She thought of her own pastor. Every Sunday he opened the Bible and taught the people. God was using the pastor's righteous, good lips to feed people God's word as he spoke. Does God use your lips to tell others God's words?

Hide and Seek Words ☐

As you read your Bible try to find these hidden words:

"It is as sport to a fool to do mischief"

A Foolish Prank

Tom and Jeff sat in the principal's office.

"Tom Murray," said the principal.

"That's the name on the wall," snarled the school custodian.

"Let's see your hands, boys," the principal demanded. Tom's hands were clean, but Jeff's had green paint on them.

The boys followed the principal and the custodian outside. On the brick wall in bold green letters was Tom's name.

"T-O-M-M-U-R-R-Y," spelled Tom. "But my last name is "M-U-R-R-A-Y!"

"When did this happen?" the principal asked the custodian.

"Between 10:00 and 10:15."

Tom had been in class then.

A very sad Jeff scrubbed the school brick wall with a toothbrush all day Saturday to remove Tom's name which he had painted on the wall! Jeff's "sport" had made him look very foolish, indeed.

Hide and Seek Words ☐

As you read your Bible try to find these hidden words:

"A talebearer revealeth secrets"

Feathers

A feather pillow contains thousands of tiny feathers. If the pillow is not sewn together tightly these leak out, and you are always picking them up.

Talebearers are like feather pillows. They let out little pieces of stories. They drop a hint here and there, but nobody can get enough of the story to learn the truth! Many lies are started by such people. The talebearer may only have a "feather" of the story himself, but he wants people to think he knows the whole thing. So he adds to the story until it is no longer true.

Next time you are tempted to tell a secret, think of taking a feather pillow up on a roof on a windy day and dumping all the feathers out. You couldn't possibly gather them all back again!

Just so, a talebearer's story, once spread around, cannot be stopped until many people have been hurt.

Hide and Seek Words ☐

As you read your Bible try to find these hidden words:

"He that troubleth his own house [family]"

A Windy Future

Tom's family was picnicking by a lake. Down the lake came a small sailboat with a man guiding it. Suddenly the sail whipped around and the boat tipped over.

"What caused that?" Tom asked his dad, as the man struggled to get his boat ashore.

"The wind changed. The breeze is pretty strong today. But," added Dad, "an experienced sailor would have steered the boat and kept the wind in the sails so it could push the boat."

Families are like boats. Tossed by storms (troubles) on the sea of life, they sometimes get upset. If family members continue to fight, the "storms" may become too much to handle, then the family may separate.

Do you want a happy family which honors God? Don't cause trouble at home.

Hide and Seek Words ☐

As you read your Bible try to find these hidden words:

"Fools make a mock at sin"

The Way the Devil Has Fun

You have probably seen people laugh when others said or did things that were wrong. This is the devil's idea of fun. God wants folks to have fun. But you are foolish to laugh at sin, for God hates sin.

God's Word says, "All have sinned," and the payment for sin is death (Romans 3:23; 6:23). But God's gift is eternal life in Heaven. To make this possible, the Lord Jesus Christ died on the cross for you (John 3:16; Romans 5:8).

If you receive Christ as your Savior you will be His child. As you follow Christ, you will hate sin as He does.

Will you be a "silly fool" or a "saved friend" of Jesus?

Hide and Seek Words ☐

As you read your Bible try to find these hidden words:

"A soft answer turneth away wrath [anger]"

Soft-Tongued Tom

Tom heard an angry shout. "Come back here," Mr. Smith yelled.

Tom wheeled his bike around. He was puffing from pedaling hard when he braked to a stop in front of the red-faced Mr. Smith. "Yes, sir," said Tom politely. "What can I do for you?"

"What's the idea of missing three of my papers this week?" Mr. Smith demanded.

"I don't know what happened, but I'll get more papers for you," Tom offered. Mr. Smith went into his house feeling better.

The next day Mr. Smith stopped Tom again. "I'm sorry I lost my temper yesterday, Tom. I've learned a dog was carrying off my paper! If you had answered me the way I spoke to you, you would have lost a customer."

Tom thought of Proverbs 15:1 as he pedaled off. He was glad his answer had been soft.

"Only by pride cometh contention [quarreling]"

What It Takes to Make a Fight

When people fight it is usually over some silly thing of little importance. According to today's verse all quarrels are caused by pride. Pride is thinking you deserve special attention. The opposite of pride is meekness. To be meek is not to demand special attention. Satan fell because of pride. In Isaiah 14:12-17, Satan boasted, "I will be like God." For this he was put out of Heaven.

Though the Lord Jesus was God, He rode on a donkey like a poor man, not on a white horse like a king. Jesus was meek. Will you be like *Him*?

Hide and Seek Words □

As you read your Bible try to find these hidden words:

"He that walketh with wise men shall be wise"

Straight Ahead

Tom's dad frowned as he read Tom's report card. "You have been tardy for school eleven times this quarter," Dad said as he looked at Tom. Dad asked his wife, "What time do you send Tom to school?"

"He always leaves in plenty of time," replied Tom's mother, sounding worried.

That evening Tom and his father made some important decisions. His mother would call the school each morning to see if Tom arrived on time. If he was tardy again his mother would walk him to school.

Tom was ashamed. Lately, he and Jeff had been walking to school with a gang of rough boys. Some of them smoked and told dirty stories. They were never in a hurry to get to school. Sometimes they didn't go at all!

Next morning when Jeff said, "Let's wait for the other guys," Tom wisely went straight to school.

Hide and Seek Words ☐

As you read your Bible try to find these hidden words:

"He that spareth his rod hateth his son"

God's Pruning

One fall day Tom was helping his dad who was busily trimming the rosebushes. Tom tied the cut branches into bundles.

"Dad," Tom asked, "Aren't these Mother's favorite roses? Why are we cutting them?"

"Son," Dad explained, "When the rosebushes get so thick that they keep out the sun, and so tall that the roots can't keep up with the leaves and blooms, we cut them back. This is called 'pruning.' Then the rosebushes will put out larger blooms next season."

Like a rosebush with too many branches which keep out the sun, your sin keeps Jesus from shining in your life. Disobedience must be "trimmed off." This is the job of your parents. Sometimes God wants them to use a rod or stick to help you obey. They do this because they love you.

God's Rules for Me

Hide and Seek Words ☐
As you read your Bible try to find these hidden words:
"And God spake all these words"

God's Rules

No teacher stayed long at Roadston's small one-room schoolhouse. The children made life so miserable for him that he was eager to leave as soon as possible. But the children were not happy either!

When Mr. Rocky Target became their teacher they soon realized he was different! The very first day he stood beside the chalkboard and explained, "Everything alive needs rules in order to live happily. The birds obey certain rules in order to build nests, raise their babies, and fly south for the winter. Ants obey rules in order to have food to eat during long winter months when the ground is covered with snow."

Mr. Target made the children feel good about having a list of rules to obey in order to have a happy school.

God has rules for us to obey, too. An important list of them is found in the second book of the Bible. These rules are called the Ten Commandments.

Hide and Seek Words ☐

As you read your Bible try to find these hidden words:

"...if thou shalt hearken [listen] diligently"

An Agreement with God

Does your dad make agreements with you sometimes? He might say, "Kelly, you may play with the boys this afternoon, but *only* after you clean up the basement."

A huge crowd of God's special people, the Jews, had traveled many days. At the foot of a rugged mountain they camped, waiting. God who had set them free from slavery was on that mountain, talking with their leader.

They had lived in a wicked country with people who worshiped many false gods. God wanted them to worship only the one true God.

The verses you read today came at the end of a long agreement God made with His people. This agreement included the Ten Commandments. God would bless them when they obeyed.

Ever since then people have been deciding whether to listen to God and obey...or not (Joshua 24:15).

Hide and Seek Words ☐
As you read your Bible try to find these hidden words:
"I can do all things through Christ"

Alone Is Too Hard

Our Bible is divided into two parts: the Old Testament and the New Testament. *Testament* is another word for *covenant* or *agreement*. When Jesus came to the world to die for our sins, that marked the beginning of God's new agreement with people.

How is the new agreement different from the old? In Matthew 5:17 Jesus tells that by His coming He wasn't destroying the old agreement, but making it possible for us to keep the agreement!

For many years people had tried by themselves to keep God's rules but hadn't been able to. Finally Jesus, God's Son, came and showed us His perfect life. He alone could keep the law as God wants it to be kept.

Now, by His Spirit, the Lord Jesus can live in YOU if you choose to belong to Him. Through His power you, too, can obey God's rules!

Hide and Seek Words ☐
As you read your Bible try to find these hidden words:

"I will . . . write it [my law] in their hearts"

Changed

Ever since six-year-old Caleb could remember he had always been told not to cross the street in front of his house.

But today his father told him, "Caleb, we've seen that we can trust you to obey us and be careful. Because you have changed, the rules can change. When your mother or I tell you to, you may cross the street."

When Jesus repeats God's rules in the New Testament they seem changed. This is because God changes you.

The biggest change that happens is when you receive the Lord Jesus as your Savior, His Holy Spirit lives inside of you. You begin wanting

to do the right things. God's rules seem to be written "in your heart." Now God can expect you, with Jesus' help, to obey Him.

Hide and Seek Words ☐

As you read your Bible try to find these hidden words:

"He . . . shall be IN you"

The Helper

"Oh, boy! Now we can quit!"

Dan and Debbie's job had been to rake up the leaves while their dad was away. Their arms were tired and the wind kept blowing the leaves from their pile. It seemed like an impossible job! When their father drove up in the car they thought they could stop.

"Oh no, don't," said Dad with a cheerful grin as he opened the car door. "Come, I'll help you now." He grabbed his giant-size rake and the three of them finished in a hurry.

•   •   •

You can keep God's rules today! He will help you by His Holy Spirit in you, like Dan and Debbie's dad helped them with the job they couldn't do alone.

But what are God's rules? In the rest of your Daily Bread booklet you will learn what the Ten Commandments mean and what Jesus says about them in the New Testament.

Hide and Seek Words ☐
As you read your Bible try to find these hidden words:
" . . . **no other gods before me**"

New Clothes!

"Thou shalt have no other gods before me" is the first of the Ten Commandments. In the New Testament this commandment is said more plainly, "You shall love the Lord your God with *all* your heart . . . ."

Are you wondering, "Will I have any love left over for my parents and friends if I love God with all my heart?"

A young beggar boy from the streets in India was to be adopted into a Christian home. He was puzzled when his new parents asked him to give them *all* his clothes. Those filthy rags were all he owned. But when he gave them up he was given a whole new wardrobe of clean clothes!

When we give God *all* our imperfect, selfish love, He takes it and puts into our hearts His perfect, unselfish love. Then we can love others as we should.

Hide and Seek Words ☐

As you read your Bible try to find these hidden words:

" . . . keep yourselves from idols"

Idols! Me?!

Terry and his father were studying the Ten Commandments.

"We don't have to worry about idols, do we, Dad?" he asked when he read the first commandment. "We don't worship idols in *this* country."

"Wait just a minute, Son," his father said. "Let's check our dictionary and see what the word *idol* or *god* means."

Terry took the heavy dictionary from the shelf and looked up the word *god*. "Dad, it says a god is a statue or image, but also a god can be any person or thing that is the chief object of one's love. What does that mean?"

"It means that your *god* or your *idol* is whatever is most important to you."

Terry looked thoughtful. "That must mean if getting a ten-speed is more important to me than anything, it is my *god*! I guess that commandment is for me today."

Hide and Seek Words ☐

As you read your Bible try to find these hidden words:

"God is a Spirit"

Not to Be Seen

"Where is God?" asked Danny, looking around. He and his father were kneeling beside his bed to pray.

"He's here, listening to us," said his father.

"But I don't see Him," said Danny.

"The Bible tells us God is a Spirit, Danny. We can't see a Spirit."

"I wish I could see Him," said the little boy.

• • •

Have you ever felt like Danny? You would like to see God when you talk to Him.

Some people want to see the one they worship so much that they *make* something they think might look like Him. But when people make something to worship, even if it is beautiful or made out of silver or gold, they do not please God at all. From the beginning God taught His people not to do this:

"Ye shall not make with me gods of silver" Exodus 20:23.

Hide and Seek Words ☐

As you read your Bible try to find these hidden words:

"Thou shalt not take the name of the Lord thy God in vain"

A Wonderful Name

"Mom!" Ginger came running into the house. "Mom, Terry has Daddy's fur-lined slippers outside and has filled them with mud!"

Terry knew better than to do that, so his mother had to punish him. He had to learn that part of loving his father was to respect what belonged to his father.

Part of loving our Heavenly Father is being respectful of what belongs to Him. His name belongs to Him like your name belongs to you. His name helps us understand who He is, so Jesus taught us to pray, "Our Father which art in heaven, hallowed be thy name." (Hallowed means *honored*.)

When we use God's name lightly or without respect we are breaking this commandment. The people in Moses' day did this by promising something "in God's name," and then not doing it.

How do you sometimes break this commandment?

Hide and Seek Words ☐

As you read your Bible try to find these hidden words:

"Let your yea [yes] be yea
and your nay [no] be nay . . ."

Watch Those Words!

Mark was having a hard time believing Joel.

"You saw an *eagle* in
the big oak by the creek?"

"I sure did! Promise you!
I swear it . . . on a stack of
Bibles!"

"Joel, come here please," called his father
from the next room.

Father and son talked a long while together.
Joel learned something new.

"God doesn't want us to have to swear in
order to get people to believe us. He wants us
to be so careful with our words that people will
trust our simple yes and no."

They read together the verses you just read.

When they had finished, and had prayed
together, Joel went back to his brother.

"Mark, it was a large bird. I'm not sure if it
was an eagle. I couldn't see it very well," Joel
admitted.

Hide and Seek Words □

As you read your Bible try to find these hidden words:

"Six days shalt thou . . . do all thy work"

A Day of Rest

God made rules because He knew we needed them. They are for our good.

Shari's Uncle Harry was very sick. The doctor told him he had been working too hard. Now he would have to be careful for many weeks until his heart was stronger. He wouldn't be able to go back to his job again.

God knows our bodies need rest. He was thinking of this when He created the world. He could have given us warm, bright daylight all the time. But, knowing our needs, He made the cool darkness so we could rest. At the same time He planned something else for our rest, one day a week was to be His day—a special day without work.

Before Jesus died, God's people had Saturday as their day for rest and worship. But after Jesus rose from the dead early on a Sunday morning, Christians began meeting together on Sunday to worship Him (Acts 20:7).

Hide and Seek Words ☐

As you read your Bible try to find these hidden words:

"Honor thy father and thy mother"

Your VIP's
(Very Important People)

God makes the command to honor (respect) your parents especially important. If you obey that command He promises you will live longer!

Jeff's little sister Beth is only one year old. His mother is very careful to keep the gate at the top of the stairs locked when Beth is playing in the hallway. Beth doesn't understand about stairs yet and could tumble down them. The gate in the yard is kept locked, too, because Beth doesn't understand about cars and busy streets. As Beth gets older her parents will use words instead of gates to try to protect her from dangers.

God gave parents to watch out for you and keep you safe from sin and danger. To obey and respect them is for your good.

Why don't you hug your parents today and thank them for taking care of you!

Hide and Seek Words ☐

As you read your Bible try to find these hidden words:

"... that it may be well with thee"

Who Is Boss?

What is obedience? The dictionary says that to obey is to yield (give in) to the authority of another. An authority is one who has the right to tell you what to do and make you do it. Do you give in to the authority of your parents?

Some people don't want anyone to tell them what to do. Absalom was a person like that. When he talked with his father, King David, he tried to force his father to change his mind about things? (2 Samuel 13).

Do you ever try to force your parents to change their mind about somethings? "Oh, Dad! Just this once ..."

Absalom never did give in to his father's authority. He died when he was still a young man, while making war against his father who loved him. His father was so sad that he cried, "My son, Absalom! If only I could have died in your place."

Hide and Seek Words ☐

As you read your Bible try to find these hidden words:

"Whosoever is angry . . ."

A Dangerous Seed!

Debbie's three-year-old brother, Kevin, was angry. Debbie had accidentally upset his tower of blocks. He threw one of his blocks at her, hoping to hit her with it.

Mother was watching. The punishment she gave Kevin was the same as if he *had* hit Debbie with the block.

•   •   •

The verses you read tell us that God's punishment for anger which makes you *want* to hurt people is no different than His punishment for killing people. You see, anger is like a seed. Murder is the plant that might come from that seed.

The Lord Jesus got angry sometimes, but He got angry about the *wrong* things people did. He still loved the people. He had no angry words for the people who were nailing Him to the cross, only, "Father, forgive them . . ."

" . . . let not the sun go down upon your wrath"

A Happy Ending

Kim was worried. "I get angry sometimes. Does that mean I might kill somebody?"

"I get angry sometimes too," her father said. "God must have known we would get angry, because He also said, 'Let not the sun go down upon your wrath.' That means, don't let the day end without getting rid of your anger."

"How can a person get rid of anger?" Kim questioned.

"There is another part of our verse. It says, 'neither give place to the devil.' Kim, you can choose to give that angry place in your heart to the devil. You do that by choosing to think about the anger. So it grows bigger . . . and bigger.

"If, instead, you give that angry place inside of you to Jesus, do you know what He might tell you to do?"

"No," said Kim.

"He might tell you to do something good for the person who made you angry. And soon the anger will melt away!"

Hide and Seek Words ☐

As you read your Bible try to find these hidden words:

"Thou shalt not commit adultery"

Your Thoughts Are You

The seventh commandment is "Thou shalt not commit adultery." Adultery happens when a married person is not faithful to [doesn't keep] the promises he made when he got married.

After God gave His rules the people often thought they were keeping them if they didn't *do* something wrong—like if they didn't actually go out and kill somebody. But when Jesus came He explained that we break the commandment, "Do not kill," even when we hate somebody.

In the verse you read today Jesus teaches us that the commandment, "Do not commit adultery" means more than the wrong things a married person might *do*. A person can sin in his heart, in his *thoughts*, where nobody sees him except God.

God tells us that we are really like what we think in our hearts (Proverbs 23:7). What are your thoughts like? Would you like to begin to obey Jesus even in your thoughts?

Hide and Seek Words ☐

As you read your Bible try to find these hidden words:

"They . . . shall be one"

Important Promises

"I do," promised Jenny's big brother Robert, standing tall and happy beside Cynthia. The wedding candles flickered as though they were happy, too. Cynthia would be Jenny's sister-in-law now.

Jenny saved her questions until after the wedding.

"Mother, did they prom-ise they would belong to each other until they die?"

"Yes, honey. A wedding is a very serious time."

"But why?" Jenny asked. "Why do they promise for such a long time?"

"Jenny, God wants a home to be a picture of His love for us. Just as God will never stop loving us, two people who marry should never stop loving each other. God makes them so they are two parts of one person."

"What God has joined together let not man put asunder [break apart]" (Matthew 19:6).

Hide and Seek Words ☐

As you read your Bible try to find these hidden words:

"Thou shalt not steal"

Can I Steal?

Stealing is taking what belongs to someone else without his permission.

There are many different ways you can steal. Did you know you are stealing when you find your friend's toy and keep it instead of returning it? Did you know you are stealing when the salesgirl by mistake gives you a dollar extra change and you don't tell her?

You can steal from people and you can steal from God. You can steal money and things. You can even steal time—by wasting it when it doesn't really belong to you.

Do you suppose you can be stealing from God if you do as you please today instead of asking what He wants you to do?

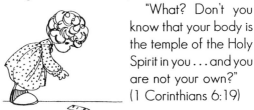

"What? Don't you know that your body is the temple of the Holy Spirit in you . . . and you are not your own?"
(1 Corinthians 6:19)

Hide and Seek Words ☐

As you read your Bible try to find these hidden words:

"He was a thief"

Little Tigers Become Big Tigers!

Once a young African boy insisted on keeping a tiger cub as a pet. The village chief kept telling him, "Little tigers become big tigers and big tigers kill!" He wouldn't believe the chief, and one day the growing tiger attacked and killed the boy.

Sins are like the tiger. They seem harmless and fun at first. What could be so terrible about taking a dime from the corner of your father's drawer? But small sins lead to bigger sins.

You remember Judas Iscariot was the man who betrayed Jesus. But did you know that long before he decided to betray Him in a big way, he must have been doing it in little ways? He was in charge of taking care of the money bag for the Lord Jesus and His disciples. Perhaps he began by stealing from the money bag a little at a time!

If it is a sin
Then it is not small
If there is a question
Don't do it at all!

Hide and Seek Words ☐

As you read your Bible try to find these hidden words:

"Thou shalt not bear false witness"

What Would You Do?

A witness is someone who has seen something or knows something, so he is able to tell others the truth about it. A false witness knows the truth, but he tells a lie instead. Sometimes a person can be a false witness by not saying anything!

•   •   •

"Sarah did it!"

"Yeah, Sarah did it!"

Sarah hadn't spilled the paint, but it was easy to blame her. She was a shy girl who wouldn't speak up for herself. Most of the children were afraid to tell the teacher that Karl had spilled the green paint on Sarah's desk. Karl was a rough, angry boy.

Were the silent children being false witnesses? _____

What would you have done if you had been in that classroom? _____

_____

Hide and Seek Words ☐

As you read your Bible try to find these hidden words:

"Putting away lying, speak . . . truth"

Do You Want This Reward?

Abraham Lincoln was a man who could be trusted to be the president of our country. Even when he was young his neighbors knew they could trust him not to lie to them.

One day when he was working at a small country store, Lincoln gave a woman less tea than she had paid for. Though tired after a day of work, he wrapped up a quarter of a pound of tea and walked four miles to her house to give it to her. He didn't want to be a false witness about the mistake he had made, even if it was a small one.

•   •   •

Your reward for being careful to obey the commandment not to bear false witness will be that people will trust you. Begin today to watch that all you say and do is true and right. Jesus will help you!

Hide and Seek Words ☐

As you read your Bible try to find these hidden words:

" . . . let us be . . . content"

Gimme!

"But Jamie has one!"

Mike's face was stormy. His eyes grew dark and the corners of his mouth pointed toward the floor. He glared at his father.

"I know Jamie has one, Son. Probably others in your class have a bicycle, too. But that doesn't mean you have to have one right now." His father's voice was sad but firm.

Sometimes we get to wanting things for the wrong reasons. Somebody else has it so we think we deserve one too. We get unhappy because we can't have it. We covet. We may think it isn't as bad as lying or stealing, but to God it is. God's people are to be a happy people. One way we can be happy is by learning to be content with what we have.

"Be content with such things as you have" (Hebrews 13:5).

Hide and Seek Words ☐

As you read your Bible try to find these hidden words:

"Do all things without murmurings"

Grumble! Grouch! Moan!

Have you noticed that often people who have the least to grumble about do the most grumbling? Do you know somebody who is hurt or sick or cannot walk—but is always smiling? Doesn't that person make you feel ashamed for having grumbled about your break-fast or about what you had to wear today?

When Paul wrote the words you read in Philippians he was a prisoner—not allowed to go anywhere alone! He was in a city far from home, far from the people who knew and loved him well. Not only that, but he didn't deserve to be in prison. He had done nothing wrong! You would think he would have a few grumbles in him somewhere—but no! Instead he writes: "I have learned . . . to be content [at peace, satisfied]."

When a person stops coveting (wanting what is not his) he has no more reason to complain and grumble. He is content.

Hide and Seek Words ☐

As you read your Bible try to find these hidden words:

"On these two commandments hang all"

Small Packages

Nathan's father brought home a food dehydrator. Together, father and son cut apples into slices and put the slices on little shelves in the dehydrator. When 28 apples had been dried, they all fit easily into two quart-size packages. How small they had become!

In case you are having trouble remembering the Ten Commandments, Jesus put them all into two commandments:

1. Love the Lord your God with all your heart, with all your soul and with all your mind.
2. Love your neighbor as yourself.

If you really love God, will you put other things ahead of Him...or make idols to worship...or take His name in vain...or not make His day special?_____

If you love other people as much as you love yourself will you be rude to your parents...hate people...steal...lie...or wish you had their things?_____

The Ten Commandments have now become two: I must love God and I must love you.

Hide and Seek Words □

As you read your Bible try to find these hidden words:

"... **love** ... **as I have loved you**"

A Special Kind of Love

What kind of love does Jesus want us to have?

Maybe you have been given a Valentine card that said, "I love you." When you gave it to a friend at school did that prove you loved him?

Love is more than what you say or write, isn't it? Love is also what you do. The verse you read tells us the kind of love we must have for God and other people. Jesus said we must love each other in the same way He has loved us.

How does Jesus show His love for you? He is patient when you make Him sad. He is kind when you need His help. He was willing to die for you on the cross. He is busy preparing a place for you in Heaven. He forgives you each day when you confess that you've done wrong.

Do you love anybody with that kind of love?

Hide and Seek Words ☐

As you read your Bible try to find these hidden words:

"Charity [love] suffereth long, and is kind"

Am I Like Jesus?

A young man, Josif, was in a communist prison with a pastor. Sometimes they talked together about Jesus. Josif said he wondered what Jesus had been like when He was on earth.

The pastor saw that Josif was cold one day. He took off his own coat and gave it to Josif. The pastor shared his food with other prisoners even when it meant he would have to go hungry. As Josif watched this man he learned

what Jesus was like. He said, "Pastor, if Jesus is like you, then I love Him, too." He believed in Jesus from then on.

People will be watching what you say and do today. Will they be able to say, "If Jesus is like you, then I love Him, too"?

Hide and Seek Words ☐

As you read your Bible try to find these hidden words:

"...**seeketh not her own**"

Seeing Another's Need

Did you ever refuse a piece of candy you really wanted to have?

One day a man in prison received a special gift—two lumps of sugar. None of the prisoners had even seen sugar for years. All of them watched this one man hungrily, wondering what he would do. He wrapped the sugar up again saying, "I shall not eat it yet. Someone might be worse off than I during the day."

He never did eat the sugar. For two years it was passed from man to man in that room. Each man saved it, thinking someone else might need it more than he did.

You learn to be unselfish when you don't just think of what *you* want and what *you* need. You think of what your tired mother needs, or your unhappy little brother, or the lonely girl in your class at school. And you try to help them.

Hide and Seek Words ☐

As you read your Bible try to find these hidden words:

"[Love] . . . beareth all things . . . endureth all things"

A Hard Thing to Do

When you come home from school and find your crayons broken and scattered, is it easy to forgive your little brother? Is it easy to forgive your mother when she accidentally blames you for something you didn't do?

All of us have a hard time forgiving those who hurt us. But forgiveness is part of the love of Jesus. Remember how He forgave those who nailed His hands and feet to the cross?

When God the Holy Spirit lives in you and you are obedient to Him, you will be able to forgive anybody, no matter what they do to you. The love you show when you forgive them will help them understand Jesus' love.

Try it today.

"For if you forgive men . . . your Heavenly Father will also forgive you: but if you forgive not men their sins, neither will your Father forgive your sins" (Matthew 6:14, 15).

Hide and Seek Words ☐

As you read your Bible try to find these hidden words:

"He shall serve him for ever"

Love-Slave

Would you like to be a slave?

"No!" you probably say.

Did you know that sometimes people have chosen to be slaves?

In Old Testament times God had planned in His law that no Jewish person could be kept as a slave by another Jew more than six years. There was one exception. If the slave honestly loved his master and wanted to always be his slave, a hole was made in his ear with a sharp instrument called an awl. He was marked as a love-slave. He had chosen to serve his master as long as he lived.

Does this help you understand what God wants you to do? He loves you and has rules He wants you to follow. Obeying them won't always be easy, but you *will* have a special happiness in your heart. You have to choose. Do you love God enough to decide to be His love-slave?

Hide and Seek Words ☐

As you read your Bible try to find these hidden words:

" . . . love is the fulfilling of the law"

One Word Says It!

    If someone asked you, "Tell me in one word what the Ten Commandments are all about." Could you? If you can, write that word here: __ __ __ __

Now check out this word for yourself:

1. If I love God will I have other gods? ___
2. If I love God will I worship other things instead of Him? ___
3. If I love God will I take His name in vain? ___
4. If I love God will I try to do what pleases Him on His day? ___
5. If I love my parents will I respect and obey them? ___
6. If I love people will I hate or kill them? ___
7. If I love the person I marry will I keep my promises to that person? ___
8. If I love people will I take what belongs to them? ___
9. If I love people will I tell lies about them? ___
10. If I love people will I be wishing I had their things? ___

God's Plan for Me

Hide and Seek Words ☐

As you read your Bible try to find these hidden words:

"I am the light of the world"

Night or Light?

Jeff was excited! Tom, Jeff's church camp counselor, was taking his group of boys for a midnight hike.

"Let's try something," said Tom. "Turn off all your flashlights and we'll hike in the dark."

Jeff didn't want to say anything, but he was afraid of the dark. He could hear the other boys stumbling along behind him. One of the boys called, "Please, Tom, we need the light."

Tom's flashlight beamed on and Jeff gave a sigh of relief. "You see how hard it is to walk in darkness?" asked Tom. "Sin is like darkness. But Jesus is the Light of the world and He can wash away your sins."

Jeff was glad for the light. He was also glad that Jesus had died for him and rose again. "Please take away my sins, Lord Jesus," prayed Jeff quietly. "I want to serve You and follow Your light."

Hide and Seek Words ☐

As you read your Bible try to find these hidden words:

"Ye are my witnesses, saith the Lord"

Living Sermons

Timmy was watching a courtroom scene on television. The black-robed judge was speaking sternly to a young man. "You must answer my question," said the judge. "You are a witness to the accident."

So that's what a witness is, thought Timmy. *A witness is a person who tells what he knows is true.*

You know that we all have sinned. To sin means to do, say or think wrong things. Because of sin, we are separated from God. We deserve to die. But God loved us so much that He sent His Son, Jesus, to take our punishment for us. If you have asked the Lord Jesus to be your Savior, then you are a witness. You should tell others what you know is true about Him. Tell them that Jesus died in their place. He will forgive their sins if they ask Him.

Will you be a witness for Jesus right now?

Hide and Seek Words ☐
As you read your Bible try to find these hidden words:

"Trust in the Lord with all thine heart"

Dedicated to God

When someone gives a lot of time and effort to a job and is careful to do his very best, we say that person is "dedicated" to his work.

To be dedicated to God means *trusting* Him with all you have, giving yourself to Him. You can trust God completely because He loves you and has promised to take care of His children. He will make the right decision for you. God never makes mistakes.

How wonderful it is to be able to dedicate, or give, your life to such a loving Father! You can serve God best when you are wholly dedicated to Him.

Hide and Seek Words ☐

As you read your Bible try to find these hidden words:

"The Lord is on my side"

What Will They Think?

With a ten-dollar bill grasped firmly in her fist, Penny skipped toward the supermarket. She recited the list of groceries her mother had sent her to buy. "Lettuce, apples, milk and—"

"Hey, Penny!" shouted a mocking voice. "On your way to Sunday school?"

Penny swung around to face the three older girls who stood by the alleyway. The Hunt sisters were known to pick fights. "N-no," Penny stammered. "I'm going to the store for my mother."

"Then you must have some money," said the oldest girl as she stepped toward Penny. "Give it to me!"

Penny wanted to run away, but she thought, *If I do that, what will they think of Jesus?* Quickly she prayed for courage and answered firmly, "No, we won't."

"We?" laughed the girl, "You and who else?"

"God," said Penny. "He's on my side." Then she turned and fearlessly skipped off to buy the groceries.

Hide and Seek Words ☐

As you read your Bible try to find these hidden words:

" . . . the robe of righteousness"

God's Coat

I remember when I got my first new coat. My old hand-me-down coat was torn and the color badly faded. But the bright, new coat! Oh, it was so soft and warm!

You know, salvation is like getting a new coat. We come to God wearing the "old coat of our own righteousness," or goodness. But we are not good enough for Heaven. We feel ashamed to stand before God because we know we've sinned.

But look! God takes away our old coat (the

good things we try to do) and covers us with *His* coat of righteousness, or goodness.

Our own righteousness is not good enough. We need God's goodness to help us live a new life that pleases Him.

Now we can serve God with all our hearts.

This is how to serve God best—
Put on Jesus' righteousness!

Hide and Seek Words ☐

As you read your Bible try to find these hidden words:

"Flee these things"

When to Run

The bright green yo-yo glistened on the front lawn as if inviting someone to pick it up! Paul was walking along the street and frowned at the shiny yo-yo. A voice inside him seemed to say, "Go ahead. Take it. No one will ever know." *God will know,* thought Paul. *Oh, but this is such a wonderful yo-yo! How would it feel in my hand?*

"Hi, Paul," said Donny, "What are you doing?"

"I'm resisting temptation," said Paul. "I want that yo-yo, but I know I shouldn't take it. So I'm just looking at it."

"That's silly!" exclaimed Donny. "The more you look at it, the more you will want it. The Bible says you should flee, or run from temptation."

"It does?" Paul asked, surprised. "I want to obey God. Let's go to my house, okay?"

The boys had so much fun playing together that Paul never even thought about the yo-yo.

Hide and Seek Words ☐

As you read your Bible try to find these hidden words:

"...my sins are not hid from thee"

Hidden Sin

"No, you may not have your allow-ance," Mother told Heather firmly. "You haven't done your chores for a week."

Angrily, Heather ran outside to the garage, grabbed her mother's packet of flower seeds, and raced to the playhouse. As she buried the seed packet, she pouted, *If I can't have my allowance, then she can't have any flowers.*

As the summer weeks passed, Heather soon forgot her anger, though she felt bad about burying her mother's flower seeds. So Heather never went near the playhouse.

Then one day her mother called, "Heather, come here!"

"What is it?" Then Heather saw where her mother was pointing. There in front of the playhouse grew a cluster of bright flowers! Mother knew! Heather listened tearfully when her mother said, "We can't hide our sin from God. But if we ask His forgiveness, He can make our sinful lives into something beautiful, just like these flowers."

Hide and Seek Words ☐
As you read your Bible try to find these hidden words:

" . . . be agreed"

In Step With Jesus

Have you ever been in a three-legged race? One person ties his left leg to another person's right leg. Then the two try to walk together. It's hard to keep walking that way in rhythm, isn't it? Sometimes one person starts walking too fast and makes the other person trip. This means that two walking together have not agreed on how fast to walk.

If we want to "walk in step" with Jesus—live pleasing to Him—we need to agree with Him. We should think the same way about things. Jesus tells us that we need His strength against sin, so we should call on Him for help. Jesus promises that He will never leave us, so we should trust Him to take care of us. See how it works? Think of some other ways you and Jesus could be agreed as you walk together each day of your life.

Hide and Seek Words ☐

As you read your Bible try to find these hidden words:

"I direct my prayer unto thee"

Talk to God

I have a friend, Kim, who is deaf. She can't hear the sound of my voice so we talk in a different way. Instead of our voices we use special positions of our fingers and hands to talk to each other. This is called sign language. Kim doesn't have to say a word to tell me what is on her mind.

This is the way prayer works, too. God can hear us even when we don't speak out loud. He hears with a special "heart language." This means He knows how we feel before we even say it!

When is the best time to pray? Some people talk to God when they first wake up in the

morning. Others like to end their day with prayer right before they hop into bed. But I think the best time to talk to God is *any* time!

Hide and Seek Words ☐
As you read your Bible try to find these hidden words:

"Teach me thy way, O Lord"

God Talks to You

If you have received Jesus as your Savior from sin, God has a special message for you. Do you know what the message is? It is the Bible! You will learn wonderful things about Heaven and your new life in the Lord Jesus.

How sad it must be for those who don't have the Bible in their own language! We need to pray for the people who are translating the Bible into different languages so that everyone can learn about God. We can also give money to help these people. God might even choose you to be a teacher of the Bible in a far-off land one day. How exciting it is to let others know that God loves them!

Pray, give, and go
So others will know.

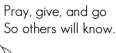

Hide and Seek Words ☐

As you read your Bible try to find these hidden words:

"Neglect not the gift that is in thee"

Use It!

Once an old man came to visit a great artist. "Would you look at my sketches and tell me what you think?" pleaded the old man.

The artist studied the drawings and sadly replied, "I'm afraid these are not very good."

The old man handed him some more sketches and said, "Please look at these."

"Ah," said the artist, "These drawings show great promise!"

With tears in his eyes the old man said, "All the drawings are mine. The good drawings were made when I was young, but I didn't use my talent. I neglected it."

Do you have a talent you can use for God? Music? Art? Love? Leadership? Friendliness? Time? Use it now. A talent is a gift from God. Ask Him and He will show you how to use your gift for Him.

Hide and Seek Words □

As you read your Bible try to find these hidden words:

"Be ye therefore ready"

Ready or Not!

Jana was always late for something. Late for the school bus. Late for parties. Late for Sunday school. Late for dental appointments. She seemed to be late for everything!

One day Aunt Eleanor came to visit. "Jana," she said, "My cousin Joan will be coming tomorrow to take me shopping downtown. If you are ready, you may come with us and ride in a taxi."

What fun! Jana was especially excited about riding in a real taxi. However, when Cousin Joan arrived, Jana was playing at the creek and was left behind.

Later that night, Aunt Eleanor held a sorrowful girl on her lap. "You couldn't come because you weren't ready, Jana. Will you be ready when Jesus comes?"

In her heart, Jana prayed, *"Dear Jesus, I want to be ready when You come. Forgive me for always being late and keeping others waiting. Help me to do better."*

Hide and Seek Words ☐

As you read your Bible try to find these hidden words:

"... grieve not the Holy Spirit"

When God Is Sad

When someone kisses you good night, you feel loved. When your favorite toy gets broken, you feel sad. When someone makes fun of your best friend, you feel angry. These feelings are called emotions.

God has emotions, too. He is happy when He sees His children treating others with kindness. But He is grieved, or sad, when His children sin.

With Jesus in your heart, you do not have to do wrong things. When you ask Jesus to wash away your sins, the Holy Spirit of God comes to live right inside you. He helps you to do right things. But sometimes you sin anyway and this makes God sad. You need to tell Him right away you are sorry and ask Him to forgive you and help you not to sin.

Hide and Seek Words ☐

As you read your Bible try to find these hidden words:

" . . . godly sorrow worketh repentance"

I'm Sorry

"Tommy! I told you not to play with my airplane!" Josh said sternly to his little brother.

"I'm sorry," said Tommy, and he ran outside to play.

The next day Josh caught Tommy playing with his airplane again. "Tommy!" Josh's yell startled Tommy. The airplane slipped from his hand and crashed to the floor.

"I'm sorry," said Tommy as he helped Josh pick up the pieces.

"You always say that," grumbled Josh.

Josh fixed the airplane and Tommy was careful never to touch it again.

"Now I know you're truly sorry," said Josh. "God really taught you a lesson in repentance."

"God taught me a lesson," agreed Tommy, "but what does repentance mean?"

Josh grinned. "Repentance means 'sorry enough not to do it again.' "

Hide and Seek Words □

" . . . singing . . . to the Lord"

Singing Hearts

Kristi was humming softly as she colored with her new crayons. Her brother Gary looked up from the book he was reading. "What song is that?" he asked.

"It's a thank-you song for my new crayons," Kristi said with a grin. "I made it up and now I'm singing it to Jesus."

Have you ever been so happy that you just felt like singing? Singing to Jesus is one way to show how much you love Him. You could sing a hymn or chorus you've learned in Sunday school. You could even make up your own song to sing to Jesus. How pleased He must be to hear His children sing to Him! Isn't singing a wonderful way to say thank You?

Hide and Seek Words ☐
As you read your Bible try to find these hidden words:

"Let all things be done . . . in order"

Neatness Counts

The Sunday school room buzzed with excitement! Courtney listened politely as the teacher, Mrs. Holmes, assigned jobs for the church program. Courtney was sure she wouldn't get a job. She wished she could do something for Jesus, but it seemed she had no talents. Karen could sing. Katie and Angela could draw. Courtney gave a little sigh. *I always do my best,* she thought, *but you can't call that a talent.* She remembered her father telling her, "Neatness counts, Courtney. Do things in order." Her father was the best carpenter in the state of Illinois. *But neatness isn't a talent,* she thought.

"And also," Mrs. Holmes was saying, "I think

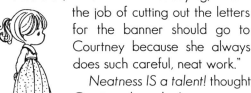

the job of cutting out the letters for the banner should go to Courtney because she always does such careful, neat work."

Neatness IS a talent! thought Courtney happily. *I can use my talent of carefulness for Jesus!*

Hide and Seek Words ☐

As you read your Bible try to find these hidden words:

" . . . giving thanks always"

Thank You, God

Joel and Jennifer ran toward Grandma. Joel held something brown carefully in his hand. "Grandma!" shouted Jennifer. "What is this thing?"

Grandma took the brown wad from Joel's hand. "Why, this is just the thing we need!" she said with a smile. "This is a praying mantis egg case. Go put it in the garden, Joel."

"You mean plant it?" asked Joel, puzzled.

Grandma laughed. "No, just lay it in the middle of the garden. When the babies hatch, they will help rid the garden of insect pests."

"God is helping us to have a better garden," said Jennifer. "Let's thank Him."

"All right," said Grandma. "You know, thanking God is one way of serving Him. We worship Him when we give thanks. It makes Him happy."

"It makes me happy, too!" said Joel.

> Serving God with thankfulness
> A happy spirit brings.
> Giving thanks for everything
> Will make a heart that sings.

Hide and Seek Words ☐
As you read your Bible try to find these hidden words:

" . . . do all to the glory of God"

A Creator? Who, Me?

To create means to make something new. When God created He made everything out of nothing! He just said the words and something new was there. When God made people, He made them in His own image. That means, like God, you have a mind that can think new ideas. You, too, can create!

Can you create something out of nothing? No, only God can do that. But you can use what God has given you to make new things. An artist makes a new p _____. A writer creates a new s _____. By showing God's special love to others you can make new f _____.

God has given you an imagination so that you can create. Perhaps you like to draw, or write stories, or make new friends. Maybe you can build or sew. Do the things you create bring honor to God? Do your creations help others know God?

Hide and Seek Words ☐

As you read your Bible try to find these hidden words:

"The earth is the Lord's"

God's Money

"Here is your allowance, Michael," said Mr. Harris.

"Thanks, Dad," Michael said as he held the dollar. "Now I have almost enough saved to buy that new kite."

"What about God's share, Mike?"

Michael stared at the dollar. "One tenth of a dollar is only ten cents. That isn't much to give to God."

"No, it isn't since the whole earth belongs to the Lord."

"Why doesn't He make us give all our money to Him?" Mike asked.

"God is not selfish and demanding," said Mr. Harris. "He wants us to choose to give because we love Him."

Michael thought a while about God's great love then he said, "I can buy the kite later. I'm going to ask God what *He* wants me to do with my allowance."

Hide and Seek Words ☐

As you read your Bible try to find these hidden words:

" . . . it is time to seek the Lord"

Time For What?

"Did you finish your Sunday school lesson, Kelsey?" her mother asked as the family trooped out the kitchen door toward church.

"No, Mom, I didn't have time," explained Kelsey, grabbing her Bible and lesson book.

Mom held the door open for Kelsey. "You had time to watch television and time to do your homework and time to play outside. But you didn't have time for God?"

"Oh, I talk to Him all the time," Kelsey said as she walked beside her mother.

"That's good," Mom said, "but the Bible tells us to seek the Lord. You need to read and study the Bible to find out what He wants you to do."

"Now I understand," Kelsey said. "God is always there when I pray to Him. He spends a lot of time listening to me. I need to spend more time listening to Him!"

Hide and Seek Words ☐

As you read your Bible try to find these hidden words:

"... continue ... in the things which thou hast learned"

Serve By Learning

You can serve God better by using the mind He gave you. He wants you to continue in the things you have already learned. If you know how to build things, learn to build them better! If you know how to read, learn to read better!

Of course, the most important things for you to continue learning are the things about Jesus. By listening carefully in Sunday school and church you can use your mind to learn more about the new life He gives to all who believe in Him.

The Bible tells us to continue, or keep on, in God's ways. Learning Scripture verses will help you. Having a Quiet Time with God helps, too. Pray and ask God to show you how to serve Him best with what you have learned. Use your mind for God!

Hide and Seek Words ☐
As you read your Bible try to find these hidden words:

"...the trying of your faith worketh patience"

Right Now!

A man stood on the railroad track, holding a lantern. Anxiously he peered into the night. He had to stop the train. The bridge ahead had been washed away by a flood. He waited and watched. Finally he heard the chug-chug of the train. His long wait was over!

Think what a terrible thing might have happened if the man had gotten tired of waiting! Many lives were saved because of his patience.

How can we become patient? It isn't easy. Patience comes through trusting God to help us with our problems. There are two things you can do when you have a problem. You can get angry and discouraged or you can tell God about it and wait for Him to work it out. Which way do you think is God's way?

Hide and Seek Words ☐

As you read your Bible try to find these hidden words:

"...I will show thee my faith"

Wanted: Living Faith

Let's pretend you are going on an ocean vacation. While you are there you never collect shells, postcards or sand. You don't even get a sunburn! When you get back, it will be hard to convince anyone that you have been to the ocean because you have nothing different to prove it.

In the same way, it is hard to convince people that you believe in Jesus if you are selfish or grouchy all the time. THAT doesn't prove you love Jesus! You need to have different works to show that you have living faith. How can you do this? Ask Jesus to help you be loving and kind. He will!

> I want to show others
> My faith every day,
> In the things that I do
> And the words that I say.

Hide and Seek Words ☐

As you read your Bible try to find these hidden words:

" . . . **do good unto all**"

Kindness Wins

Mike and Robby did their best to get Scott to come to the Bible club. They told him about the terrific stories and songs. But even the thought of refreshments didn't work. Scott just wasn't interested.

Imagine Mike and Robby's surprise when, that week at Bible club, who should show up but Scott!

"What made you decide to come, Scott?"

"Her," he said pointing.

"You mean Rachel?" asked Mike. "She's so shy, she won't even play games with the other kids."

"When I dropped my books, she helped me pick them up," said Scott. "And once she shared her lunch with me."

Mike and Robby looked at each other as Scott walked off. "I guess we never thought of being friends with Scott," said Robby.

"Rachel did," commented Mike. "Because of her kindness, Scott might come to know Jesus as his Savior!"

Hide and Seek Words ☐

As you read your Bible try to find these hidden words:

"Set a watch, O Lord, before my mouth"

Mouthguards

In football, it's important to wear a mouthguard. This protects the player's mouth from injury. Those who don't wear mouthguards sometimes end up with missing teeth!

Some of us need to wear "heavenly mouthguards" to guard our *words!* The unkind words we say can hurt other people. God is unhappy when His children say things that hurt or anger others. The Bible says that the tongue is like a wild animal that cannot be tamed by man. Only God can tame our tongues. We need His help. If we ask Him, He will put a guard, like a heavenly soldier, to watch the words we

say. When we are angry, God will help us not to say bad words. He will guard our mouths against saying untrue things about others. Then we can be better servants of God.

Hide and Seek Words ☐

As you read your Bible try to find these hidden words:

"...forgiving...as God...hath forgiven"

He Doesn't Deserve It!

With her chin stuck out stubbornly, Ashley walked home from school with Lisa.

"I tell you Jon tripped me on purpose!" Ashley stormed. "Look at this! My best jeans are torn where I fell on the sidewalk!"

"But he said he was sorry," Lisa comforted. "He even gave you his cookies at lunchtime. You should forgive him."

"He doesn't deserve it! Forgiving him would be too easy," Ashley said. "He needs to be taught a lesson."

"God didn't try to teach us a lesson," Lisa said quietly.

"What do you mean?" Ashley asked.

"Remember when we both asked Jesus to come into our hearts? God forgave us our sins even though we didn't deserve it. We need to forgive others just like God forgave us," Lisa answered.

"You're right, Lisa. Since God forgave me, I guess I can forgive Jon."

Hide and Seek Words ☐

As you read your Bible try to find these hidden words:

"... by love serve one another"

Being a Servant

Ryan scooted beside Uncle Wally on the bench at the kitchen table. "What are you doing?" Ryan asked.

"I'm busy being a servant," Uncle Wally answered.

"You are?" questioned Ryan. "Why, you're just writing a letter."

"But this is a very special letter," answered Uncle Wally. "I'm writing to my cousin who is in the hospital to help cheer him up."

Ryan looked puzzled. "How is that being a servant?"

"Well, God said we are to serve others by love," replied Ryan's uncle.

"I get it!" Ryan said. "We are really serving God when we help others by our love. In that case, Uncle Wally, I'll mail your letter for you. I want to start being a servant for God right now!"

Hide and Seek Words ☐

As you read your Bible try to find these hidden words:

" . . . look . . . also on
the things of others"

Others

While Jesus was on earth, He did many good things for others. He set an example to follow.

How can we think more about others? Suppose someone forgets to bring lunch money to school. Do you think Jesus would want you to offer to share your lunch with that person? Of course! When you borrow something, are you careful to return it in good condition? If you saw another child stealing something that belonged to someone else, would you stop him?

We need to be careful about hurting the

feelings of others, too. The Bible tells us to take care of others. We can take good care of their feelings by letting Jesus control us so we won't hurt them.

Hide and Seek Words ☐

As you read your Bible try to find these hidden words:

" . . . he brought him to Jesus"

Come and See

"But WHY won't you come to the Bible club meeting with me?" pleaded Todd as he followed Andrew into his room.

"Because it'll be boring," Andy answered. "Maybe you think all that singing and storytelling is exciting, but I don't."

"You've never been to a club meeting," Todd said. "You might like it. Why don't you just come and see?"

Andy sighed. "Oh, all right. But just this once."

There, for the first time, Andy learned that he was a sinner and that his sin kept him from being friends with God. The teacher said that Jesus, God's Son, died to take the punishment for sins. That day Andy asked God to forgive him of his sins.

Afterwards, Todd took Andy to talk to the teacher. "This is Andy," Todd said. "I brought him to Jesus!"

Andy's face was beaming. "I'm going to find someone to bring to Jesus, too!"

Hide and Seek Words □

As you read your Bible try to find these hidden words:

"Well done, good and faithful servant"

God's Plan Is Service

Do you truly want to hear God say to you the Hide and Seek words? If you have trusted Jesus as your Savior, you will not be punished for your sins. They are all forgiven. Some day when you stand before God He will judge the things you have done. Do you seem to be kind just so others will like you? Do you boast about giving money to missionaries? Are you proud because you think you are better than people who steal or do worse things?

To be a good and faithful servant, you must first accept Jesus as your Savior from sin. Then He will teach you how to be His servant. He wants to fill you with His love so you will be happy to help others whenever you can. You will want to do good things because you love God.

My Body, God's House

Hide and Seek Words ☐

As you read your Bible try to find these hidden words:

**"For I [God] have created
him for my glory"**

Why Are We Here?

God who made the heavens and the earth also planned and made the bodies we live in. When He created the first man and woman, He said, "Let us make man in our image." He planned and made our bodies so we can see, hear, walk, work, talk and think. God knew all about us even before we were born.

Why did God make us? The answer is found in our Hide and Seek words—for His (God's) glory. He wants us to use the bodies which He made for us to please Him and bring honor to Him. That means you should use your hands, feet, eyes, lips, mind—all of yourself to please God.

Are you doing this?

As you have your Quiet Time with God each day, He will show you how to bring honor or glory to Him.

Hide and Seek Words ☐
As you read your Bible try to find these hidden words:

"I will praise thee"

How God Made Us

One day when Susan came home from school her dad met her at the door. He said, "I have a surprise for you, Susan. You have a brand new baby brother!"

Susan was so excited. She could hardly wait for the day when mother would come home from the hospital with the baby.

When she first saw her brother, he was not very big. He had very tiny feet, hands, mouth, ears and eyes. But he didn't stay tiny—he began to grow and grow. His eyes began to notice everything. One day his lips said some words. His hands took hold of Susan's fingers. His feet began to walk. With his heart he loved his big sister. As Susan watched him grow she could see how wonderfully God makes us.

Only God could make a body like yours. That is why the Hide and Seek words say, "I will praise thee."

Have you thanked God for your body?

Hide and Seek Words ☐

As you read your Bible try to find these hidden words:

"And the child grew . . ."

The Lord Jesus' Body

When the Lord Jesus, God's Son, was here upon the earth, He had a body too. The Bible tells us He was born in Bethlehem and He grew up as a boy in Nazareth.

Was His body like ours? Let's see what the Bible says. Look up these verses:

John 4:6   Jesus was t_____ .

Mark 4:38   Jesus was a_____ .

Luke 5:13   Jesus put forth His
              h_____ .

John 19:28   Jesus was t_____ .

Yes, the Lord Jesus had a body like ours, but there was one difference. He was the perfect Son of God and He had no sin. Our minds want to think bad things; our lips want to speak naughty words and our hearts and wills want to have their own way.

The Lord Jesus loves us and came to earth to save us from sin. Is He your Savior?

Hide and Seek Words ☐

As you read your Bible try to find these hidden words:

"...bare our sins in his own body on the tree"

The Lord Jesus' Body Was Hurt for Us

"God so loved the world that he gave his only begotten Son." Jesus' body suffered and died on the cross for our sins. He did this because He wants us to be with Him in Heaven someday.

The Bible says, the payment or wages of sin is *eternal death*—to be apart from God forever. The Lord Jesus loved us so much He willingly came to take our punishment for sin, so that we could have *eternal life*—to be with God for-ever.

A jailer once asked the missionary Paul, "What must I do to be saved?" Paul answered, "Believe on the Lord Jesus Christ and thou shalt be saved." Do you know that you have a sinful heart? Tell God about it. Believe in your heart that the Lord Jesus died for you and ask Him to come in and forgive your sin.

Did you?

Hide and Seek Words ☐

As you read your Bible try to find these hidden words:

"...ye are not your own"

Not Your Own

To whom do you belong? Your parents? Your teacher? Your country? Maybe you are thinking, *I belong to myself.* What does the Bible say? "You are not your own." That means you belong to someone else. Who is that someone else? The Lord Jesus Christ.

Jesus bought you with a price when He died on the cross for your sins and rose from the grave. Because He did all this for you the Bible says, "Glorify God in your body." How can you glorify God with your body? You can dress your

body, use your body, feed your body and take care of your body in ways that honor and please Him.

The day you received the Lord Jesus as your Savior you became His child. You are not your own. You are His. Isn't that wonderful?

Hide and Seek Words ☐

As you read your Bible try to find these hidden words:

"... the Spirit of God dwelleth in you"

A Dwelling Place

Fill in the blanks below with the following words:

(1) loves (2) only (3) sins (4) gave (5) life (6) we (7) eternal (8) came (9) help (10) Lord

God (1) _ _ _ _ _ us and sent His (2) _ _ _ _ Son to die on the cross for our (3) _ _ _ _ .

Jesus Christ (1) _ _ _ _ _ us and (4) _ _ _ _ His (5) _ _ _ _ for our sins that (6) _ _ might have (7) _ _ _ _ _ _ _ life.

The Holy Spirit (1) _ _ _ _ _ us and (8) _ _ _ _ to live in us to (9) _ _ _ _ us live for the (10) _ _ _ _ Jesus Christ.

Before the Lord Jesus went back to Heaven, 40 days after He rose from the grave, He made a promise. He promised to send the Holy Spirit to live in each believer. He comforts, guides, teaches and helps us to please and honor the Lord Jesus Christ. Will you let Him do these things for you?

Hide and Seek Words ☐

As you read your Bible try to find these hidden words:

**"...present your bodies
a living sacrifice"**

A Living Sacrifice

Tom was reading his Bible and came to our verse today. "Mother, what does the word *beseech* mean?" he questioned.

Mother explained, "The word *beseech* means *to earnestly plead or beg.* Tom, the missionary Paul was writing to Christians in Rome when he said these words. He was begging them to give their bodies to God to serve Him because God was so good to them."

Mother continued. "God also wants very much for *us* to give our bodies to Him as a living sacrifice. To be a living sacrifice means we will be willing to be what God wants us to be, to do what He wants us to do and to go where He wants us to go. This is the way we show our love to Him for all He has done for us.

"Have you told God you want your life to be a living sacrifice, Tom?"

"No, but I want to right now, Mother."

WHAT ABOUT YOU?

Hide and Seek Words ☐

As you read your Bible try to find these hidden words:

"...it was pleasant to the eyes"

Be Careful Little Eyes

Josh was hungry. He had nothing to eat since breakfast and it was almost supper time. Hurrying home he passed an open market. Oh! Those peaches looked so good. No one was around, so he took one. What happened? Josh was *not* careful how he used his eyes.

Eve, in the garden of Eden, looked at the forbidden tree and saw that it was good for food. She saw that it was beautiful to look at. Eve took of the fruit and ate it. She was not careful how she used her eyes and so she sinned by disobeying God.

Sin often comes into our lives because of what we look at. The Bible calls it "the lust, or desires, of the eyes."

Oh, be careful little eyes what you see

There's a Savior up above

And He's looking down in love,

Oh, be careful little eyes what you see.

Are you being careful?

Hide and Seek Words ☐

As you read your Bible try to find these hidden words:

"... the seeing eye, the Lord hath made"

Use Your Eyes to Please God

God made our eyes. They are wonderfully made and sight is very precious. We should use our eyes to please God.

Here is a quiz. Which of these things will please the Lord, when you do them? Cross out the wrong ones.

Use Your Eyes...

1. To read the Bible
2. To study your school lessons
3. To watch television when you should not
4. To see beautiful things in nature
5. To look at someone's paper during test time
6. To read dirty comic books
7. To read to Grandma or someone sick
8. To look at bad movies
9. To watch someone hurt another person
10. To look for cars before crossing the street

Prayer—Thank You God for my eyes. Help me to use them to please You. Amen.

Hide and Seek Words ☐

As you read your Bible try to find these hidden words:

" . . . speak for thy servant heareth"

Be Careful Little Ears

"Mike," Father shouted, "where are your ears"? Quickly Mike felt on both sides of his head. "Why! They're still here! Why did you ask me that?" This may seem funny but Father had been talking to Mike and he was not hearing. He had good ears but he was not listening. Our ears are sometime like radios. We can turn them off and on!

The boy Samuel in the Bible had his ears turned on! When God called him one night, he answered, "Speak, for thy servant heareth." Samuel listened and God told him many things and blessed him (gave him good things).

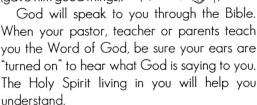

God will speak to you through the Bible. When your pastor, teacher or parents teach you the Word of God, be sure your ears are "turned on" to hear what God is saying to you. The Holy Spirit living in you will help you understand.

Hide and Seek Words ☐

As you read your Bible try to find these hidden words:

"Hear, ye children;
the instruction of a father"

Listen for God

What you see and hear is what you think about. What you think about is often what you do! So it is very important that you hear and see good things.

Are you filling your mind with things that do not please God? Are you listening to dirty stories, lies and loud music that make you think wrong thoughts and do wrong things? God's

enemy, Satan, is also your enemy. He knows you belong to the Lord Jesus Christ and he will do all he can to keep you from listening to and obeying God.

God has given us His Word, the Bible, to instruct us in doing right. He has given us the Holy Spirit to teach us and help us do what the Bible says. Has God given you a father who loves God to show you how you should live?

Are you listening for God and obeying Him?

Hide and Seek Words ☐

As you read your Bible try to find these hidden words:

" . . . the tongue is a little member"

Be Careful Little Tongue

The Bible warns you to be careful how you use your tongue in speaking. The tongue is a very little member of your body, but if it is not controlled by God it can be used to say things that may do great harm. The Bible says the tongue is like a fire! It only takes one little match to start a fire that can spread and destroy many things. So, one little word can start a fight and before it is over someone may have gotten hurt very badly. The Bible says a soft answer (kind words) turn away anger.

David, who wrote the beautiful Psalms in the Bible said, "Let the words of my mouth . . . be acceptable [pleasing] in thy sight, O Lord" (Psalm 19:14).

This would be a good prayer to pray each morning, don't you think?

Hide and Seek Words ☐

As you read your Bible try to find these hidden words:

"My lips shall praise thee"

Use Your Lips for God

The little maid who worked in Naaman's home used her lips to say words that pleased the Lord. Though she was a captive in a strange land and perhaps very lonely for her father and

mother, she was not afraid to tell Naaman's wife about her God. She was sure that God was able to heal Naaman of his sickness. This brought honor to God for Naaman was healed and he began to serve the true God.

It takes courage to speak for the Lord Jesus Christ. He wants you to be a witness—to tell others about Him. Perhaps some of your friends do not know that the Lord Jesus died for their sins. He would be pleased for you to be the one to tell them.

Praise the Lord with your lips—speak kindly, cheerfully, respectfully and honestly.

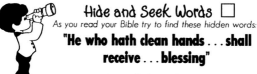

Hide and Seek Words ☐

As you read your Bible try to find these hidden words:

"He who hath clean hands . . . shall receive . . . blessing"

Be Careful Little Hands

I washed my hands this morning,
So very clean and white
And gave them both to Jesus
To work for Him till night.

I told my ears to listen
Quite closely all day through,
For any act of kindness
such little hands can do.

My eyes are set to watch them
About their work or play
To keep them out of mischief
For Jesus' sake all day.

The Lord Jesus wants us to have clean hands, not only clean because they have been washed with soap and water, but because they are clean from sin and do the things that please Him.

Here is a good rule to follow for using your hands—

"Whatsoever you do, do it heartily [the best you can] as to the Lord . . ." (Colossians 3:23).

Hide and Seek Words ☐

As you read your Bible try to find these hidden words:

"What is that in thine hand?"

Use Your Hands for Jesus

The Lord Jesus has a work for each one of us to do today. We all have something in our hands we can use for Him.

Moses used his shepherd's rod.

David used his slingshot.

Gideon used his clay pitcher.

Dorcas used her needle.

What about you? What do you have in your hand?

A rake to clean the yard?

A bicycle with which to do errands?

A helping hand to help some older person across the street?

A pen to write a letter?

A dollar to put in the missionary offering?

A cloth with which to do the dusting?

What do you have in your hand that you can use for the Lord Jesus? Write it on this line.

_____.

Hide and Seek Words ☐

As you read your Bible try to find these hidden words:

" . . . beautiful are the feet of them that preach the gospel"

Be Careful Little Feet

Sarah was hurrying just as fast as she could. She could not walk very fast. She was almost there when her pastor came walking beside her. "Sarah," he said, "you have beautiful feet." Sarah stopped. She looked at her feet and then at the pastor with questioning eyes.

"My feet are ugly," Sarah replied, "they are not beautiful." You see, Sarah was crippled. Both her feet were crooked. "How can you say they are beautiful?" she asked.

Pastor Parker looked down at her and said kindly, "God says they are beautiful because you use them for Him. You visit the sick, you do errands for older people, you come faithfully to meetings at church. Though your feet are crippled, God sees them as beautiful."

You may have good feet and can walk and run well, but can God say your feet are beautiful?

Hide and Seek Words □

As you read your Bible try to find these hidden words:

"Thy word is a lamp unto my feet"

Little Feet Be Careful

Our feet often get us into mischief, don't they? They kick your sister under the table and make her cry. They trip someone on the way to school. They go to a ball game instead of coming right home. They sneak to be with the gang rather than go to a church club. Yes, we use our feet to get us into a lot of trouble.

Have you ever walked in the dark using a

flashlight to see where you were going? Step by step you could see as the flashlight shone ahead.

God's Word is like a light or lamp to your feet to show you the right way to live. As you read and hide God's Word in your heart the Holy Spirit will show you good places to go and the right things to do. This is the way to keep your feet out of mischief.

Hide and Seek Words ☐

As you read your Bible try to find these hidden words:

"The Lord knoweth [our] thoughts"

Be Careful What You Think

It was Sarah's eighth birthday. She was so excited! "Would Mother remember? Would she make a cake?" Sarah's mind was working fast that morning.

At breakfast Mother said nothing about Sarah's birthday but hurried her off to school. Sarah was disappointed. She began to think *Mother doesn't love me. Mother is too busy to think about me.*

All day Sarah thought these wrong thoughts until she became very unhappy. She pouted all the way home. To her surprise, Mother was waiting for her. In the dining room were seven of her friends and a beautiful cake on the table! How ashamed Sarah was of her thoughts.

Did God know what Sarah was thinking all day? Yes. He knows all things, even the deepest secrets of our hearts.

Ask the Lord Jesus to put the right thoughts in your mind today.

Hide and Seek Words ☐

As you read your Bible try to find these hidden words:

" . . . **think on these things**"

Follow God's Rules

God in His Word, the Bible, has given us rules to keep our thoughts pleasing to Him. Let's see what they are!

Whatever things are

true
honest
just (right)
pure
lovely
of good report
praise to God

Think on These Things

God's Word is true, honest, just, pure, lovely, gives a good report and praises God. Does this give you a clue about what to think of each day? Yes, learning and hiding God's Word in your heart and mind is a good way to have right thoughts.

Prayer: Lord Jesus, help me to follow Your rules for good thoughts. Amen.

Hide and Seek Words ☐

As you read your Bible try to find these hidden words:

"Trust in the Lord with all thine [your] heart"

Trusting is Believing

Trust is another word for *believe*. When you sit on a chair you believe or trust the chair is strong enough to hold you. When you switch on the light you believe or trust that the light will go on.

To trust the Lord with *all* your heart means to believe and trust that He will do *all* He has said and promised in His Word, the Bible.

If you have trusted Him to be your Savior, you also need to trust Him to keep you from sinning each day. Trust Him to take care of you and help you in all you have to do.

Faith is another word for trust and believe.

> Faith is just believing (trusting)
> What God says He will do;
> He will never fail us,
> His promises are true,
> If we but receive Him
> His children we become;
> Faith is just believing (trusting)
> This wondrous thing is done.

Hide and Seek Words □

As you read your Bible try to find these hidden words:

"...love the Lord...with all thy heart"

Love Him!

We love those we trust.

To love the Lord Jesus with all your heart means to love and trust Him above everybody and everything. He must be first in your life.

The Lord Jesus loves us. He left His wonderful home in Heaven to come to earth. He took a body like ours, though He had no sin. He lived here and died on the cross for our sins and rose again so He could be our Savior. Someday He will take us to Heaven to be with Him.

"We love him [the Lord Jesus], because he first loved us" (1 John 4:19).

Hide and Seek Words ☐

As you read your Bible try to find these hidden words:

**"Precious . . . are thy
thoughts unto me, O God"**

We are Precious to God

If you could change something about yourself,
what would it be? The color of your eyes or hair?
To be taller or shorter? What would it be?

Did you know that you are special to God
just as you are? He made
you and me and each of us
special. Not one of us has
even a thumb print alike. You
are one of a kind.

You are not only special
in the way you look but also
in what you can do. God has given each of us
a talent to do something for Him. It could be to
sing, speak, cook, care for the sick, fix cars, pilot
a plane, be a policeman or many other things.

God's thoughts are precious toward you
because He made you. Do not wish to be
changed. Thank the Lord He made you as you
are. Then, use the special talent He has given
you to serve Him!

Hide and Seek Words ☐

As you read your Bible try to find these hidden words:

" . . . a certain nobleman whose son was sick"

Your Body Can Hurt

I am sure you have said, "Why do I have to be sick?"

In our Hide and Seek words today, we learn that a certain nobleman's son was sick. Sickness comes to everyone, children, grownups, rich or poor. We do not have perfect bodies. They often hurt. Why! Because of sin.

Adam and Eve, the first man and woman, had perfect bodies when God made them. They had no headaches, measles, earaches or anything else. Everything was wonderful. But when sin came into the world by their disobedience, God said their bodies would be weak and one day even die. Ever since that time there has been sickness and death.

If you have received Jesus as your Savior, someday in Heaven you will have a perfect body. Until then God wants you to take care of your body, because it is the house in which His Holy Spirit lives.

Hide and Seek Words ☐
As you read your Bible try to find these hidden words:

"... he would not defile himself ... with the king's meat"

Not Only Candy

Jennifer loved candy. She begged Mother many times a day for a piece. Sometimes she even took a piece without asking. At mealtime Jennifer wasn't hungry and didn't drink her milk nor eat her food as she should. She became sick and was in the hospital a long time.

Our bodies belong to God. He wants us to take good care of them. One way to do this is to eat the right kind of foods—not only candy. When Mother says, "drink your milk and eat your vegetables," you should obey.

In the Bible, we read that Daniel decided in his heart not to eat the rich food from the king's table. It was not good for his body and it was offered to idols. Instead he asked for plain food like vegetables and water to drink. God blessed him because he chose to do this.

Hide and Seek Words □

As you read your Bible try to find these hidden words:

" . . . **come** . . . **rest a while**"

Oh, No! Not Yet!

The Lord Jesus had gathered His disciples (helpers) together. They had much to tell Him for they had just come back from preaching in other cities. They told Him all they had done and what they had taught. They were tired and needed to rest. The Lord Jesus knew this, so He said, "Come aside into a desert [quiet] place and rest a while."

Your body, too, needs rest. At the end of the day you are tired. Isn't it wonderful God has given you the quietness of the night to sleep and to gain new strength for the next day? Have you

ever thanked God for rest and sleep?

What do you answer when Mother or Father says, "It is bedtime." Do you say, "Okay," or "Oh, no, not yet"?

Hide and Seek Words ☐

As you read your Bible try to find these hidden words:

"Bodily exercise profiteth a little"

Exercise

We all want to grow, don't we? None of us want to stay small and weak. There are three rules we need to keep in order to grow. What are they?

1. Eat the right food
2. Get enough rest
3. Exercise

Exercise is good for you. It makes your body strong. Boys especially like to have strong muscles. They exercise each day to build them up.

You should not only want your *body* to grow but your spiritual life as well. How do you grow as a Christian?

Read the Bible—that is your food

Pray each day—that is your rest

Tell others about the Lord Jesus—that is your exercise

Prayer—Dear Heavenly Father, help me to take care of my body and help me to grow in my Christian life, too. In Jesus' name, Amen.

Hide and Seek Words ☐

As you read your Bible try to find these hidden words:

"...beholding his...face in a mirror"

What Does the Mirror Say?

Has Mother ever said to you, "Go look in the mirror"? Why? Did she want the mirror to tell you something?

We know mirrors do not talk, but they can tell you your face is dirty or your hair needs combing.

If your body belongs to the Lord Jesus and the Holy Spirit lives in it, shouldn't you keep your body clean?

God not only wants you to be clean on the outside but also in the inside. God's Word is like a mirror for your heart and mind. It shows you

the hate, lies, and wrong thoughts in your heart just like a mirror shows your face is dirty.

To keep clean on the outside and inside, obey the mirror on the wall *and* the mirror of God's Word!

Hide and Seek Words ☐

As you read your Bible try to find these hidden words:

" . . . do all to the glory of God"

What Will I Wear?

Katie was having a real hard time deciding what dress to wear to Lisa's party. The red one? The white one? If only Mother was here to help. Then she thought, *I will ask the Lord Jesus to help me decide.* She bowed her head and prayed.

Is the Lord Jesus interested in what you wear? Yes. Have you ever prayed about what you should wear? The Hide and Seek words tell

you to do all to the glory (honor) of God—even the way you dress.

I'm sure you want to honor the Lord Jesus and let others know you belong to Him. How can you do this? You can do this not only by what you say and do but how you dress. The Holy Spirit who lives in you will help you.

Hide and Seek Words ☐

As you read your Bible try to find these hidden words:

" . . . we shall all be changed"

In the Twinkling of an Eye

How long does it take to wink your eye? Not very long, does it?

Something wonderful is going to happen. The Lord Jesus is coming again. He will come in the "twinkling of an eye." When? We do not know. It may be today! Jesus is coming in the air to take all those who belong to Him to Heaven.

When Christ comes, in the twinkling of an eye, your earthly body will be changed to a body that can live in Heaven. That body will never die!

Are you ready for Jesus' coming? Is He your Savior? If not, receive Him today and be ready.

Hide and Seek Words ☐

As you read your Bible try to find these hidden words:

" . . . we shall be like him"

A New Body

Becky is a little girl who was born blind. She has never seen her mother's or father's face. She has never seen a flower, a tree or a lake. Is she unhappy? No! Why? Because she has the Lord Jesus as her Savior. God has given her a lovely voice. She sings for Him and makes many people happy.

In Heaven everyone will have a perfect body. There will be no sickness, pain or death in Heaven. No one will be blind, crippled or deaf. Each person will have a body like the Lord Jesus.

In this little book you have read about the body you now live in. You learned that God made you, Jesus bought you and the Holy Spirit lives in you. Take care of your body. Use it to please God.

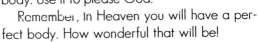

Remember, In Heaven you will have a perfect body. How wonderful that will be!

Understanding My family

© PMI

Hide and Seek Words ☐
As you read your Bible try to find these hidden words:

"God setteth the solitary [lonely] in families"

What Is a Family?

When God created you, He knew you would be very lonely if you had to live all by yourself. He knew you would need to have special people with whom you could share your thoughts, ideas and feelings. He knew you would need to be loved and be able to love others. Because you have these needs God put you in a family!

A family is a group of people who are related to each other. They live and grow up

together, learning to love and care for each other. God wants to use the experiences you have at home and the lessons you learn in your family life to help you grow up and please Him.

Hide and Seek Words □
As you read your Bible try to find these hidden words:
" . . . the Lord built the house [family]"

The First Family

The family is God's idea! The family is the first form of human government.

Remember back in Gensis, the first book of the Bible, how God created Adam and gave him the special task of being in charge of (governing) the land and the animals all around him? When Adam told God how lonely he was, God gave him a wife who was to be Adam's helper and friend. Adam and Eve had their home in the beautiful garden of Eden. God blessed them and told them to have children. Adam was instructed by God to be the leader of his family.

Throughout the whole Bible we read stories about people and their families. The Bible tells us about God's plan for the family and the special opportunities and responsibilities each family member has.

Dear Heavenly Father,
Thank You for Your plan for the family;
Help me to understand my special place
in my family. Amen.

Hide and Seek Words ☐
As you read your Bible try to find these hidden words:

"Honor thy father and mother"

God's Plan

God has a wonderful plan for the family. In God's plan your parents have been placed in authority over you, just as God is in authority over your parents. Your parents are responsible to God to give you the love, guidance and discipline you need in order to grow up to be what God wants you to be. Therefore, you must respect (honor) your parents as the very ones that God was chosen to watch over you.

God's plan for Moses' life was very special; he was to lead the Israelites out of the land of Egypt. God needed just the right person to discipline and train Moses for this task. God chose Moses' own mother for this purpose. (Exodus 2)

God has a special plan for your life and He has chosen your parents to prepare you for this plan.

Think about this:

Being what God wants me to be begins with obeying my parents!

Hide and Seek Words ☐

As you read your Bible try to find these hidden words:

" . . . children of God by faith"

God's Family

Nicodemus was an important leader of the Jewish people. He lived at the time Jesus was on the earth. One night, perhaps so he would not be seen by the other Jewish leaders, Nicodemus went to talk to Jesus. Nicodemus had a question that was troubling him.

Nicodemus asked, "What do you mean, I have to be born all over again?"

God has a family—a family of all the people who have faith in Jesus, God's Son, and received Him as their Savior. Just as you were born into your parent's family, you must be born into God's spiritual family. That's why Jesus told Nicodemus, "Ye must be born again" (John 3:7).

To be born into God's family, you must believe that Jesus died on the cross for your sins and ask Him to be your Savior.

For God so loved (put your name here) that He gave His only begotten Son that if (put your name here) believes on Him, he/she shall not perish but have everlasting life. (John 3:16)

Hide and Seek Words ☐
As you read your Bible try to find these hidden words:

"The Lord is . . . not willing that any should perish"

For All Who Believe

Your Heavenly Father has an eternal blessing (a good thing that will last forever) He wishes to give to every person in your family. It is the blessing of knowing that all your sins are forgiven and that you will "not perish, but have everlasting life." (Remember John 3:16?)

If your parents are not already Christians, ask the Lord Jesus to help them become Christians by being born into God's family.

Happy the home where Jesus' name
Is sweet to ev'ry ear;
Where the children all learn how great
   is His love
Where parents hold Him dear.

Hide and Seek Words ☐

As you read your Bible try to find these hidden words:

" . . . faith that is in thee"

A Christian Family Is Special

Timothy was a young man who came to know Jesus as his Savior through the preaching of the apostle Paul. Timothy came from a Christian family and grew up knowing his mother and grandmother had faith in God. Even though Timothy was born into a Christian family, he still had to be born again into God's spiritual family.

Growing up in a Christian family is very special. Christian parents and grandparents can guide you and pray for you. Timothy's mother and grandmother were good examples and helped him become strong in faith. Thank the Lord today for Christian parents and grandparents.

Hide and Seek Words ☐

As you read your Bible try to find these hidden words:

"Children are a heritage [gift] of the Lord"

You Are Special

Hannah prayed that she might have a child, for she knew that a child is a special gift from God. When her son was born she named him Samuel which means "asked of God." Samuel was very special to his mother (1 Samuel 1:20).

You, too, are a gift from God to your parents. God has given you to them to bring joy to their lives and to help them become what God wants them to be. You are a perfect gift, even though there may be things you do not always like about yourself. (Read James 1:17.)

It is important for you to believe that you are special to your parents and God. God has made you according to His careful plan. Will you thank Him?

THINK ABOUT THIS:
If you like yourself,
others will like you, too!

Hide and Seek Words ☐

As you read your Bible try to find these hidden words:

" . . . train up a child in the way he should go"

When Parents Say "No"

Samson, the strong man in the Bible delivered the Israelites from their enemies. He did the special task God gave him to do, but Samson didn't obey all the instructions of the Lord. Because he did things *his* way instead of God's way, it cost him his life to get the job done.

Did you ever wonder why Samson had difficulty obeying the Lord?

When Samson was a child, it seems as though his parents had trouble telling him "No." Because he did not learn to obey his parents, he did not learn to obey God.

I wonder if you obey when your parents say, "No." This is God's way to teach you obedience to Him. It is important training for when you grow up!

Hide and Seek Words ☐

As you read your Bible try to find these hidden words:

"He that spareth the rod hateth his son"

Spankings and Blessings

The sons of Eli were evil (bad) men who didn't love the Lord. Although Eli was a priest in God's temple, he was not faithful to God in disciplining his sons. Because he didn't punish his sons when they were naughty, they never learned how to live pleasing to God. (Read 1 Samuel 2:12.)

Although it doesn't always seem like it, your mom and dad are showing you they love you when they punish you for being naughty. They are correcting your behavior for you now so that when you grow up you will be able to correct your own behavior.

God, our Heavenly Father, also shows His love to us when He corrects us. "For whom the Lord loveth, he chasteneth [corrects]" (Hebrews 12:6).

> Dear Heavenly Father:
>
> It's awfully hard to say this, but,
>
> Thank You for spankings that show me
>
> I am loved. Amen.

Hide and Seek Words ☐

As you read your Bible try to find these hidden words:

"...obey your parents in all things"

Obedience Tested

Isaac was Abraham's only son and Abraham loved him very much. As Isaac grew up, he was taught to obey his parents. Isaac trusted his father and obeyed him without questioning.

One day God decided to test Abraham to see if he loved God as much as he loved his son, Isaac. God told Abraham to offer Isaac as a sacrifice to Him. Abraham obeyed his Heavenly Father without questioning, just as Isaac obeyed him. Read the story in Genesis 22. Find out how God provided a sacrifice in Isaac's place (Genesis 22:13).

You may not always understand the reason why your parents ask you to do something, but to please the Lord you must obey. God blesses children who obey their parents!

THINK ABOUT THIS:
When I obey my parents, I am also obeying God.

Hide and Seek Words ☐
As you read your Bible try to find these hidden words:
"Even a child is known by his doings"

The Family Mirror

Daniel was a Jewish prince whose parents had carefully trained him according to the Jewish law. He was a fine young fellow. In the first chapter of Daniel, we find Daniel was taken prisoner into Babylon—far away from his parents, where he was free to behave any way he wanted. Daniel could have said, "Wow, at last I'm free! I think I'll act just like the Babylonians." But Daniel refused to disobey what he had learned at home and God took care of him in this strange land. Once He even kept Daniel from being eaten by lions!

Dear Heavenly Father;
I never thought of it this way before.

I am like a family mirror.
I reflect the things I learn at
    home.
Help me, dear Lord, to show,
    like Daniel,
That I was taught to do right.
                    Amen.

Hide and Seek Words ☐
As you read your Bible try to find these hidden words:

"...bringing into captivity every thought"

Captive Enemy Thoughts

There are many unkind thoughts and feelings that can become your enemies if you do not learn to "capture" them or keep them from growing. Satan, your spiritual enemy, wants your thoughts and feelings to turn against others so you will hurt them instead of loving them.

Satan especially likes to see wrong feelings make trouble in your family. He knows how important your family is in helping you follow God.

Dear Heavenly Father...
Just as the boy David defeated the giant,
With Your help and one small stone;
Help me capture my unkind thoughts and
Think loving ones instead. Amen.

Hide and Seek Words ☐

As you read your Bible try to find these hidden words:

"...and his brethren [brothers] envied him"

Envy Hurts

Joseph's older brothers envied him because their father had given Joseph a beautiful coat.

"Why, Father never gave US beautiful coats," they complained. I imagine they went on to say, "All of us have always wanted a coat just like that. Father just isn't fair." (Remember the story in Genesis 37?)

There will always be reasons why you can envy your brother or sister. Perhaps your sister gets better grades in school than you do, or maybe your brother is a better athlete than you are. When brothers and sisters envy each other, the entire family is upset.

God has given you just what *you* need to make you happy. How do you think it makes God feel when you want something else?

THINK ABOUT THIS:

You feel envious only when you think about what you don't have instead of what you do have!!!

Hide and Seek Words ☐

As you read your Bible try to find these hidden words:

". . .and be ye thankful"

Stop It Right Away

Jealousy is much like envy. It begins with little feelings like: "My brother is luckier than I am because he gets everything he wants" or, "my sister thinks she is so smart because she won first place in the swimming race."

You feel jealous when you think about what you don't have and when you compare yourself to others (especially your brother or sister). You must be very careful not to let jealously grow in your life. There is one sure way to stop it—be thankful for the things you DO have! Be thankful for the special abilities God has given you. Be thankful for God's special plan for your life.

"In everything give thanks..." (1 Thessalonians 5:18).

Hide and Seek Words ☐

As you read your Bible try to find these hidden words:

"Trust in the Lord with all thine heart"

The Bad Twins

One day, Caleb and Tim were playing at home while their mother had gone to the grocery store. Suddenly, they thought they heard a noise. The more they thought about it, the more certain they were that they were hearing a very strange noise. They began to worry and wonder when mother would get home. By the time mother returned, the boys were very frightened and worried.

Fear and worry are like twins. They often come together and easily get out of control. Your imagination helps these twins grow bigger and stronger. They can grow so big that they cause you to be grouchy and say things to your family you don't really mean.

The Lord Jesus does not want you to be afraid and worried. He wants you to trust Him to take care of you. The fear and worry will go away when you trust the Lord Jesus.

"Casting all your care upon him;
for he careth for you" (1 Peter 5:7).

Hide and Seek Words ☐

As you read your Bible try to find these hidden words:

"...ye fathers, provoke not your children to wrath"

The Red-Faced Monster

Many years before you were born, God knew that sometimes your father would come home from work tired and irritable, and that sometimes he wouldn't be as patient with you as he could be. That's why God has given a warning to fathers, "Be careful not to keep after your children until they become angry."

God also knew that you would sometimes become angry with your father. Everybody feels angry at times. But anger can easily become a sin if you do not let God control it. Even if someone else irritates you or does wrong to you, God holds you responsible for your anger.

A prayer for you:

Dear Heavenly Father,
Help me to stop blaming other
people for my angry feelings.
Amen.

Hide and Seek Words ☐

As you read your Bible try to find these hidden words:

"Be ye angry, and sin not"

Extra Energy

Have you ever been so angry that you ran to your room and slammed the door? At the time you were angry, did you have lots of extra energy?

God has created our bodies in such a way that when we experience strong feelings, we have lots more energy to put to use. God made us this way so that we can protect ourselves in dangerous situations. The problem is, we want to use all that energy to hurt or get even with mother and father, or brothers and sisters. Our verse for today says that when we are angry it is not right to sin, to use our energy wrongly.

Dear Heavenly Father,
Please control me when I feel angry
So that I will not sin against anyone
in my family. Amen.

Hide and Seek Words ☐

As you read your Bible try to find these hidden words:

**" . . . let not the sun go down
upon your wrath"**

You Must Decide

God says, "Don't let the day end without getting rid of your anger."

Angry feelings don't just go away. Each time you feel angry, ask God to help you make the right decisions about your angry feelings so that you will not hurt your family.

The first thing you must decide when you feel angry is that you won't act out your feeling. (To act out your anger is to *do* something—like hit your brother!) The second thing you must decide is that you will talk about your feeling. Can you learn to sit down with your brother or sister who has irritated or hurt you and tell him or her how you feel? Ask them to pray with you about it.

THINK ABOUT THIS:
Today's little angry feelings grow into Tomorrow's big angry feelings.

Hide and Seek Words ☐
As you read your Bible try to find these hidden words:
" . . . he is faithful . . . to forgive us"

No Excuses

There are all kinds of excuses to offer when you don't trust God to help you get rid of anger. You can say, "I just made a mistake," or perhaps, "I goofed." But, do you know what God calls it when you use anger wrongly? God calls it sin.

The Bible says that when you sin, you must confess that sin to God. (Confess means to admit to the Lord what you did wrong and tell Him you are sorry.) When you confess your sin, God has promised He will forgive you.

Dear Heavenly Father:
Help me to remember, my angry
   feeling may not be wrong;
but I'm always wrong when I do or say
   something unkind.
Thank You for forgiveness.

Hide and Seek Words ☐

As you read your Bible try to find these hidden words:

"Confess your faults one to another"

An Urgent Signal

"Brad," called Mother, "Have you seen that dollar I left on the table? I just can't seem to find it."

Brad's heart began to beat very fast. He had taken the dollar and spent it!

Have you ever felt terribly guilty? You can always recognize that miserable feeling. It comes when you know you've done something wrong and are not willing to admit it. The guilt will grow even stronger if you tell a lie to cover up for what you have done.

God does not want you to go through life feeling guilty; that's why He has provided forgiveness for you. The feeling of guilt is a signal to remind you that you need to confess your sin and receive forgiveness.

Brad needed to confess and receive forgiveness from both his mother and the Lord Jesus.

Hide and Seek Words ☐

As you read your Bible try to find these hidden words:

" . . . forgiving one another"

Forgiving—Forgiven

"Susie, you broke another one of my favorite toys!" complained Mary, Susie's older sister. "I'll . . . I'll never forgive you."

An important lesson that must be learned is how to forgive. Brothers and sisters are often careless in the way they treat each other and each other's belongings. So within your family you have many opportunities to learn to forgive.

What does it mean to forgive? To forgive means not to feel or act badly toward someone because of what he has done to you. It even means not to think about it again! Finally Mary asked God to help her forgive Susie for breaking her toy. She just treated her sister as though the toy had never been broken!

Jesus said that unless you are willing to forgive others, your Heavenly Father will not forgive you (Matthew 6:14-15).

Hide and Seek Words ☐

As you read your Bible try to find these hidden words:

" . . . **love one another:
for love is of God**"

Love Is of God

Love is a word that is often misused today. "Love" is used to describe how a person feels about anything from chocolate ice cream to feelings about one's parents.

God wants you to learn to love within your family. You learn to love by being loved. As you feel the love of your parents toward you, you learn to love others.

Love is more than a feeling; love involves action. When you love another person, you do everything you can that is best for him.

The Bible says that love is of God. Because God wants the very best for you He sent His Son, the Lord Jesus, to be your Savior.

Hide and Seek Words □

As you read your Bible try to find these hidden words.

" . . . love one another"

Loving—Loved

Did you know that the Lord com-manded us to love one another? The Lord expects us to love each other and to show that love. When you show love to others, they often will show love to you.

The most difficult place to show love is right in our own homes with the people to whom we are the closest. It seems as though we often hurt the ones we love the very most. The apostle Paul had the same problem. He found it hard to do the things he should do and easy to do the things he shouldn't do (Romans 7:19). But he thanked God that He would help him do right through the Lord Jesus.

Paul said . . . "I can do all things through Christ" (Philippians 4:13).

Write three ways you can show love to your family:

(1) _____

(2) _____

(3) _____

Hide and Seek Words ☐

As you read your Bible try to find these hidden words:

"It is more blessed to give"

Sharing and Blessings

There was a young boy who had packed his lunch because he was going to be away from home all day. He knew he would get hungry. Carefully carrying this lunch, he joined a crowd of five thousand people who were listening to what Jesus had to say. Soon his tummy began to grow; he was, indeed, hungry!

Just then Andrew, one of Jesus' followers, tapped him on the shoulder.

"Son, would you share your lunch with Jesus?" (You can read what happened when the boy shared in John 6:5-14.)

Sharing is an important way to show love to your family. Is there something you could share right now?

Hide and Seek Words ☐
As you read your Bible try to find these hidden words:

" . . . and be ye kind one to another"

A Two-Way Street

To be kind means to be thoughtful, gentle and considerate. In other words, if I am kind I will think of what others need before I think of what I need. If I am kind I will care about what happens to others and will do what I can to help them. The Bible says that God is kind even to those people who never say thank you and who are evil, doing bad things. (Luke 6:35) God expects you to show kindness to your parents, brothers and sisters.

THINK ABOUT THIS:
Kindness is like a two-way street:
When you show it to others,
Some kindness you will meet!
What kindness have you given at home
    today?

Hide and Seek Words ☐

As you read your Bible try to find these hidden words:

"Do all things without murmurings and disputings"

Chores, Chores, Chores

"Mom, why do I always have to clear the table?" complained Lisa.

Have you ever complained because you were expected to help around the house? Do you have chores at home for which you are responsible? The Bible says that we should do *all* things without complaining and arguing.

Your parents have two important reasons for giving you chores to do. First of all, you are a very important member of your family and your help is necessary!! Second, unless you learn to be responsible for chores at home, you will have difficulty completing tasks in school and work when you are older. You are being prepared for your own future life.

Can you thank your parents for caring enough about you to expect your help around the house?

Hide and Seek Words ☐

As you read your Bible try to find these hidden words:

"Bear ye one another's burdens"

Two to Carry Half the Load

Mother had just returned from the grocery store. The car was full of heavy grocery sacks. Just then Jeff rode up on his bike.

"I'll help you carry those groceries, Mom," he announced as he hopped off his bike. "If I help you, then you will have half as much work to do."

To bear someone else's burden means that you help that person carry a heavy load. The load may not be something you carry with your hands. A burden may be a problem at home, a lot of chores or perhaps a tough school assignment. Sometimes you can give direct help as Jeff did. At other times you can help best by showing thoughtfulness and kindness to the other person. One other important way you can bear another's burden is to pray for that person. In order to have a happy home, each family member must learn to recognize and help bear each other's burdens.

Hide and Seek Words ☐
As you read your Bible try to find these hidden words:

"If we walk in the light . . . we have fellowship"

Fellowship: A Goal

To have fellowship within your family means that you enjoy being together. You feel loved and accepted, and are able to share your thoughts, feelings and ideas with one another. When there is a feeling of fellowship between the members of your family, you can enjoy sharing many fun times together.

Fellowship, however, is not something we always have; indeed, fellowship can easily be lost. The Bible says that in order to have fellowship with God, we must walk in the light. We walk in the light by obeying God's commands.

Write in three things you can do to help keep fellowship in your family:

(1) _____

(2) _____

(3) _____

Hide and Seek Words ☐

As you read your Bible try to find these hidden words:

"And God blessed Noah and his sons"

Blessings and More Blessings

How good the warm sunshine and the cool breeze must have felt as Noah walked down the huge gangplank of the ark. Thankful to God for the way He had taken care of them, Noah called his family together, built an altar, and worshiped God (Genesis 8:15-22).

One of the most wonderful blessings a family can have is to share together in worship and prayer. God desires the fellowship of your family. He wants to have first place in your home.

God wants to bless your family just as He blessed Noah and his sons.

Dear God,
    Thank You for my family.
    Thank You for supplying our needs,
    And listening to our prayers.
    Thank You for the fellowship with You.
    Thank You for all Your blessings.
    Amen

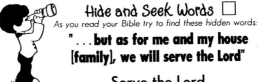

Hide and Seek Words ☐

As you read your Bible try to find these hidden words:

**" . . . but as for me and my house
[family], we will serve the Lord"**

Serve the Lord

After the death of Moses, Joshua was appointed by God to be the leader of the Jewish people. To Joshua was given the honor of leading the Jewish people into the promised land. Joshua knew that the Jewish people were having difficulty remaining true to the living God. They were often attracted to the false gods of their neighbors.

"But as for me and my family," Joshua boldly announced, "we will serve the Lord."

God wants families today to be true to Him and serve Him. God wants families to show the love of God to their neighbors by the way they live together. He wants families to serve Him by having fellowship with each other and with God. God blesses families who serve Him; God wants your family to serve Him.

Dear Heavenly Father,
Help me to do my part,
So that my family
Can serve You. Amen.

God's Ways in Our World

Hide and Seek Words ☐

As you read your Bible try to find these hidden words:

"...I will guide thee"

The Parakeet Tree

How would you like to see a parakeet tree? In St. Petersburg, Florida you can see one. Oh, it's not a tree that grows parakeets, but, every day at sundown hundreds of brightly colored birds fly to a special tree where they spend the night.

Now, the sun sets at a different time each day. How do the people in St. Petersburg know when to come and see the birds? They check

the newspaper to see when the sun will set. But how do the birds know when the sun will set? The Bible says they fly by the wisdom of God! (Job 39:26)

What about you? Are you living by the wisdom of God, letting Him guide you? He promises to show you the right way. Read today's verse again.

Hide and Seek Words ☐

As you read your Bible try to find these hidden words:

" . . . the Lord built the house [family]"

The First Family

The family is God's idea! The family is the first form of human government.

Remember back in Gensis, the first book of the Bible, how God created Adam and gave him the special task of being in charge of (governing) the land and the animals all around him? When Adam told God how lonely he was, God gave him a wife who was to be Adam's helper and friend. Adam and Eve had their home in the beautiful garden of Eden. God blessed them and told them to have children. Adam was instructed by God to be the leader of his family.

Throughout the whole Bible we read stories about people and their families. The Bible tells us about God's plan for the family and the special opportunities and responsibilities each family member has.

Dear Heavenly Father,

Thank You for Your plan for the family; Help me to understand my special place in my family. Amen.

Hide and Seek Words ☐

As you read your Bible try to find these hidden words:

" . . . **be wise**"

Wise, Working Ants

Come with me to South America and watch these little creatures work! Watch them nip off and prune back the vines, bushes and other plants from that big tree.

What creatures are we talking about? Ants!

Ants? Doing all that hard work? Yes. Did you read your verse for today? God wants you to think about how ambitious ants are. Scientists tell us that if these ants are removed from the tree it is soon overrun by other plants, and it dies. It's a good thing these ants aren't lazy!

God is not happy with us when we are lazy. Are you too lazy to do a good job on your homework? Or when your mom asks you to do the dishes? Are you lazy about witnessing?

Go to the ant
Consider her ways
Then work for Jesus
All of your days.
                    P.R.

Hide and Seek Words ☐

As you read your Bible try to find these hidden words:

" . . . working with our own hands"

Poor Bug?

"Look over here, kids," Dad called. "It's an emperor moth coming out of his cocoon."

Jeremy and Jessica came running and exclaimed, "Oh, look how hard he's pushing. Let's help the poor thing! We could make a cut in the opening so he could just slide out real easy."

"No," Dad answered, "the moth would crawl out all right but he would have a swollen body and little shriveled wings! You see, God intended him to have a struggle getting out. As he pushes through that narrow opening the pressure forces juices into his wings which give them strength.

"And, do you know something, kids? God didn't intend that life should all be easy for you either. He knows that hard work makes strong bodies—so let's get back to raking those leaves!"

Hide and Seek Words ☐

As you read your Bible try to find these hidden words:

"Teach me thy way, O Lord"

The Fish That's Not a Fish

Did you know that a whale is not a fish? Oh, it swims like a fish. But it's not born from eggs like a fish; it's born live like a mammal. And, it must put its nose out of the water to breathe.

Some whales are 14 feet long when they are born and drink 1 ½ tons of milk a day. What an appetite!

The moment the baby whale is born the mother whale must push it to the surface of the water to breathe or it will drown. Who teaches the mother whale to do this? God does.

God will guide you, too, if you'll ask Him. Read His Word and talk to Him every day. When He shows you what He wants you to do, thank Him for guiding you.

Hide and Seek Words ☐

As you read your Bible try to find these hidden words:

"As an eagle"

Mean Mother?

Do you remember the first time your mother made you clean up your room without any help? Or do the dishes? Or wash your own hair?

One day Mother told Jan, "I won't have time to help you clean your room since we are going to have company." My, you would have thought she was the meanest mother in the world!

"I can't do that all by myself," Jan pouted.

That's probably why the baby eagle squawks as his mother pushes him out of his nest. But that's the only way he'll ever learn to fly! The mother eagle stirs up her nest and makes those little birds fly so they will grow up to be strong.

You must begin now to do difficult things so you will be strong to serve the Lord.

Hide and Seek Words ☐

As you read your Bible try to find these hidden words:

" **. . . follow after righteousness** "

Leapin' Lizards?

Some children who live in Southern Florida enjoy catching little green lizards that run around outside. Do you know what happens when you try to catch a lizard by the tail? He runs away from his tail, leaving you holding it! He doesn't mind giving up his tail to save his life.

In the Bible we read a story about Joseph. One day a lady tried to get Joseph to do something he knew God wouldn't want him to do. (Genesis 39) So, when she grabbed his coat the Bible says, "he left his garment in her hand and fled [or ran] . . . ."

When Satan tempts you to do wrong, do like the lizard and Joseph—run! How do you run from sin? Tell the person who tempts you, "No, I can't do that," then ask Jesus to help you follow after righteousness (do good).

Hide and Seek Words ☐

As you read your Bible try to find these hidden words:

"Confess your faults"

Don't Hide

"When I was a little girl I lived at Sand Point, New York. What a good name that was, since we were surrounded by sandy beaches. In Sand Point there were as many turtles as there were lizards in Florida!

"I used to pick up a turtle and say, "Hello there!" He would just pull in his head and hide in his shell."

When you have an argument with a friend, do you run home and say, "I'll never play with you again"? Or do you say, "I'm sorry, let's make up and be friends"? This is what the Bible means when it says, "confess your faults."

Don't be like the turtle
And draw in your head.
Confess your faults each
    day
And make friends instead!

Hide and Seek Words ☐
As you read your Bible try to find these hidden words:

"Be watchful . . . for I have not found thy works perfect before God"

Watch Out

Carrie and her dad were walking through the woods behind their home. "Careful Carrie, don't step there. That's a snake."

"A snake? Where?"

"Right there in the pile of leaves."

Carrie looked at the pile of leaves she had almost stepped on. Sure enough, there, coiled in the leaves was a poisonous snake. A copperhead!

"Dad, I almost stepped on him!" Carrie cried as she cautiously stepped backward.

"His colors blended so perfectly with the leaves it was hard to see him. Carrie, Satan sometimes does that too. He makes lying, stealing or mean pranks look like fun so we don't see the evil that they really are."

Don't be fooled by Satan's camouflage (cover-up).

Hide and Seek Words ☐

As you read your Bible try to find these hidden words:

" . . . before the cock crow"

Cocky Crow

Have you ever heard someone say, "Now, don't act cocky!" Have you ever seen a cock? A cock is a very showy bird with a fancy tail. He struts around like he thinks he's pretty great—king of the barnyard! That's why when someone is acting like he thinks he's pretty great, people say, "Don't be cocky!"

Peter, Jesus' disciple, was so sure he would never let Jesus down. But one day Jesus said to Peter, "You will deny me before the cock crows." Peter did deny that he even knew Jesus—three times! Then a cock crowed! Peter

sadly remembered that he did wrong.

When you are tempted to think you can always do right yourself, remember the cock and ask Jesus to help you!

Hide and Seek Words ☐

As you read your Bible try to find these hidden words:

"Even a child is known by his doings"

The Family Mirror

Daniel was a Jewish prince whose parents had carefully trained him according to the Jewish law. He was a fine young fellow. In the first chapter of Daniel, we find Daniel was taken prisoner into Babylon—far away from his parents, where he was free to behave any way he wanted. Daniel could have said, "Wow, at last I'm free! I think I'll act just like the Babylonians." But Daniel refused to disobey what he had learned at home and God took care of him in this strange land. Once He even kept Daniel from being eaten by lions!

Dear Heavenly Father;
I never thought of it this way before.

I am like a family mirror.
I reflect the things I learn at
    home.
Help me, dear Lord, to show,
    like Daniel,
That I was taught to do right.
                    Amen.

Hide and Seek Words ☐

As you read your Bible try to find these hidden words:

"Jesus Christ the same"

He Never Changes

Did you ever hear the rhyme,
Red sky at night,
Sailors delight.
Red sky in the morning,
Sailors take warning.

It's true, if the sky is bright red when the sun sets in the evening it will be a nice day the next day. But, if it's red in the morning it will be a stormy day. Jesus Himself said this in Matthew 16:2, 3.

People have depended on this sign for thousands of years because God made it that way. You can always depend on Him. He never changes.

Some of your friends may disappoint you. Do you have a friend who is not kind to you anymore? Friends change, don't they? But, Jesus Christ is the same, always. Just as we have sunrise and sunset every day, so God stays the same every day. All through your life, trust God to take care of you and He will!

Hide and Seek Words ☐

As you read your Bible try to find these hidden words:

"...**in the storm**"

Are You Afraid?

On the tiny island of Bonaire stand some, not so tiny, radio towers. A missionary station uses these to send the Gospel to many people who have never heard that Jesus died on the cross for their sins.

There are wires, hundreds of feet above the ground, strung between the towers. These wires became coated with salt, blown there by the wind off the salty Caribbean waters. If the missionaries didn't get the salt off the wires they would break! It would be very dangerous to climb up there to wash them. The missionaries prayed. The Lord answered their prayers by sending the strongest rain storm they had ever seen to wash the wires!

God controls our weather. Remember that the next time you are afraid during a thunder storm, tornado, or other "bad" weather. The Lord has His way in the whirlwind and in the storm!

Hide and Seek Words ☐

As you read your Bible try to find these hidden words:

" . . . weeks of the harvest"

How Old Are You?

How old are you? How do you know? Because you were born 9 or 10 years ago? Who decided how long a year should be? God did!

The Bible says that God made two great lights, "the greater light to rule the day, and the lesser light to rule the night . . ."

The rotation (turning) of our earth divides the days, the moon going around the earth gives us months, and the earth traveling around the sun gives us years. God knew we needed a system of time. It helps us know when to plant, the weeks of the harvest, and how old we are! Isn't God good!

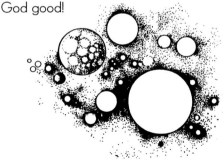

Hide and Seek Words ☐

As you read your Bible try to find these hidden words:

" . . . **born again**"

Happy Birthday!

Aren't you glad God created a system for months and years as well as days and nights? Just think how confusing it would be if someone asked you how old you are and you had to say, "I'm 3,650 days and nights old!"

Soon Ruthie will be one year old in God's family. Just one year ago she asked Jesus to be her Savior from sin.

She said, "I'm sorry I've done wrong things, Jesus. Thank You for dying on the cross for my sins. I'm glad You rose up from the grave and are alive today. Please forgive me for the wrong things I've done. Thank You for saving me."

Jesus is Ruthie's Savior and some day she can live forever in Heaven with Him as a part of God's family.

How old are you in God's family? If you have never received the Lord Jesus won't you pray Ruthie's prayer right now?

Hide and Seek Words □

As you read your Bible try to find these hidden words:

"... we are his workmanship"

Snowflakes

Have you heard that no two snow-flakes are alike? You could spend all day looking at snowflakes under a microscope and no two would be alike. Could you think up that many designs? Only God could!

There's a song called, "You're Something Special." And you are! God created only one person exactly like you and that's you!

Why did God make you just as He did? He made you to love Him and serve Him. You are His workmanship.

Can you sing? Sing for Jesus.

Can you play a musical instrument? Do it for Jesus.

Do you have a nice smile? Use it to win friends and tell them about Jesus.

Hide and Seek Words ☐

As you read your Bible try to find these hidden words:

"Hope deferred [put off]"

Promises, Promises!

Hundreds of years ago God made a promise. He put a beautiful rainbow in the sky and told Noah, "I will never again destroy the world with a flood." Every time you see a rainbow you can feel thankful that God keeps His promises.

Have you ever said, "I'll clean my room as soon as this program is over, Mom—I promise!" And then you forgot. It happens all the time, doesn't it?

When you make a promise to someone he might say to himself, "Oh, good, I hope he really does it!" But, when you don't do it his hope is deferred (put off until later) and he feels sad. Be sure when you say, "I promise," you really mean it!

Hide and Seek Words ☐

As you read your Bible try to find these hidden words:

"... let not the sun go down upon your wrath"

You Must Decide

God says, "Don't let the day end without getting rid of your anger."

Angry feelings don't just go away. Each time you feel angry, ask God to help you make the right decisions about your angry feelings so that you will not hurt your family.

The first thing you must decide when you feel angry is that you won't act out your feeling. (To act out your anger is to *do* something—like hit your brother!) The second thing you must decide is that you will talk about your feeling. Can you learn to sit down with your brother or sister who has irritated or hurt you and tell him or her how you feel? Ask them to pray with you about it.

THINK ABOUT THIS:
Today's little angry feelings grow into
Tomorrow's big angry feelings

Hide and Seek Words ☐

As you read your Bible try to find these hidden words:

"Great is the Lord, and greatly to be praised"

Salty Praises

Jerry was about to swim in the ocean for the first time. He dove into a big wave and came up licking his lips and frowning.

"Hey, Dad, this stuff tastes salty! How come?"

Dad waded out to Jerry and explained, "It's another one of God's great plans, Son. Salt keeps the earth's largest bodies of water from freezing. If the oceans and the seas froze over, the earth would become one solid piece of ice. The salt helps control the earth's weather."

"Wow, God thought of everything, didn't He Dad?" Jerry smiled.

"Yes, our God is a great God. We should praise Him (tell Him how great we think He is) for this great ocean we are enjoying."

Jerry dove into the next big wave and as he felt the ocean water bubble around him he prayed, "Thank You, God, for this wonderful world You made for us!"

Hide and Seek Words ☐

As you read your Bible try to find these hidden words:

"I can . . . through Christ!"

The Winner!

Kim was born with one normal arm and one arm which grew only as far as her elbow. Do you think Kim sat around and cried a lot about that? No, she just said, "I'll have to work twice as hard with the one hand I have."

When Kim got to high school she decided she would like to learn how to type. The typing teacher didn't know what to do with a girl with only one hand so he kept saying, "I'll teach you later."

Kim got tired of waiting so she taught herself. She practiced hard at home too. By the end of the year, Kim won a typing contest!

Kim says, "God is my helper. He has always helped me to do well even with just one hand. I know that I can do all things through Christ who helps me."

Hide and Seek Words ☐

As you read your Bible try to find these hidden words:

"Fear not"

Fear Not!

Are you afraid of the dark? Tim used to be afraid, but one day he decided to trust the Lord even in the dark. Here's how it happened.

Tim had a clock over his desk. Its long pendulum went back and forth to make the clock run. Every morning when he woke up he found the clock had stopped! Tim thought someone was sneaking into his room at night. He was afraid. He could feel his heart pounding from fear.

Then, one day Tim saw his kitten, Charlie, playfully watching the clock. Zap! Out went his paw and stopped the clock. Tim sat on the edge of his bed and thought.

How dumb of me to lay awake every night feeling afraid when all the time it was just a little kitten! From now on I'm going to just trust God to take care of me—even in the dark!

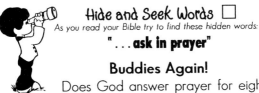

Hide and Seek Words ☐

As you read your Bible try to find these hidden words:

" . . . ask in prayer"

Buddies Again!

Does God answer prayer for eight-year-old girls?

Susan says, "Yes."

She and her dad had been motorocyle "buddies." Every Sunday morning they took long rides together.

Then, someone invited Susan to vacation Bible school. She went and loved it. She asked Jesus to be her Savior. After she received Jesus she wanted to learn more about Him. She gave up her Sunday morning rides with her dad and began to go to Sunday school. Susan learned that what she would ask in prayer, believing, God would do. She began to pray that her dad would ask Jesus to be his Savior.

Later her dad said, "I felt empty inside when I saw Susan get on that bus and ride off to Sunday school. I knew I should be going with her." So he did! And he received Jesus as his Savior. God answered Susan's prayer.

Hide and Seek Words ☐

As you read your Bible try to find these hidden words:

"... pray one for another"

Little Joel

Little Joel was born with many physical problems. He was so sickly he was put into a nursing home (like a hospital). When he was

about six months old he weighed only 9 pounds. Most babies that age weigh about 18 to 20 pounds. He couldn't sit up or even hold his head up.

One day a family who loved the Lord Jesus decided to adopt Joel. They took him home and asked the children at a Christian school to pray for him. The children prayed every day.

Now Joel is gaining weight. He is able to crawl around. He smiles a lot and is trying to talk and walk.

Will you take a moment to pray for someone who is not well? God is pleased when we pray one for another.

Hide and Seek Words ☐

As you read your Bible try to find these hidden words:

" . . . **not ashamed**"

The Bible "Nut"

Robin had moved and would have to go to a new school. She wondered, "Should I carry my Bible to school, or not?" Robin decided she would.

The kids teased Robin. "Hey, what are you, some kind of a 'nut,' bringing a Bible to school?"

Robin took the teasing with a smile and did make several friends at school. When her friends had problems they somehow knew that the girl with the Bible could help them find answers. One girl whose parents were getting

a divorce, came to tell Robin about her problem. Robin's mother was able to help the girl receive the Lord Jesus.

Robin was so glad she had not been ashamed to carry her Bible to school.

Hide and Seek Words ☐

As you read your Bible try to find these hidden words:

" . . . my ways"

What a Great Day!

God answers your prayers—but not always your way!

Matt was bored. At breakfast he prayed, "Lord, I don't have anything to do today. Please let Mike come over."

Confidently, Matt called Mike. Mike's mother answered, "I'm sorry, Matt, but Mike has the measles and can't play."

Discouraged, Matt went outside. "What a miserable day this is going to be." Just then he heard a crash. Mr. Oaks across the street looked horrified. A shelf in his garage had crashed down with nuts, bolts and nails scattered everywhere.

Matt ran to help. They worked for an hour cleaning up the mess. But Mr. Oaks was interesting to talk to and the time went by fast. Matt learned that Mr. Oaks had been a magician. He put on a full magic show for Matt! It was a great day after all!

"Thank You, Lord, that You don't always answer my prayers the way I ask You to."

Hide and Seek Words ☐
As you read your Bible try to find these hidden words:

" . . . a clean heart"

Jesus, Friend of Sinners

Greg had a problem. He had a strong desire to take things which didn't belong to him. His own mother called him a thief!

When his friend Jeff invited him to Good News Club he said, "No, I'm too bad to go. I've heard that you pray and learn about God there. That's no place for me! I do bad things all the time—just can't seem to help it."

"You may not be able to help yourself," Jeff answered, "but Jesus can help you. He died on the cross to pay for our sins. He paid for yours, too, and He wants to forgive you and help you. He said He'd give you a clean heart."

"Neat! Then I'll come to your club," Greg said.

And he did!

Hide and Seek Words ☐
As you read your Bible try to find these hidden words:

"Bear ye one another's burdens"

Two to Carry Half the Load

Mother had just returned from the grocery store. The car was full of heavy grocery sacks. Just then Jeff rode up on his bike.

"I'll help you carry those groceries, Mom," he announced as he hopped off his bike. "If I help you, then you will have half as much work to do."

To bear someone else's burden means that you help that person carry a heavy load. The load may not be something you carry with your hands. A burden may be a problem at home, a lot of chores or perhaps a tough school assignment. Sometimes you can give direct help as Jeff did. At other times you can help best by showing thoughtfulness and kindness to the other person. One other important way you can bear another's burden is to pray for that person. In order to have a happy home, each family member must learn to recognize and help bear each other's burdens.

Hide and Seek Words ☐
As you read your Bible try to find these hidden words:

" . . . ask and ye shall receive"

A Friend for Tim

Tim lived in Florida for several months but still had not found a buddy. There was no one his age in the neighborhood. He complained, "I wish we could move back to Michigan."

"Why don't you pray for a special friend?" his mother suggested.

"It wouldn't do any good. There's not even a house for sale that kids might move into around here."

"Tim, Jesus wants you to tell Him your problem," his mom answered.

Tim did pray about it. The next day his mother was standing at the door talking to a neighbor girl, when she saw a boy Tim's age walk by.

"Who is that boy?" she asked.

"That's my brother, Mark. He just stays home and reads all day!"

For the next three years Tim and Mark were buddies.

Jesus is waiting, oh do not delay.
Jesus is waiting, to hear you pray.

Hide and Seek Words ☐

As you read your Bible try to find these hidden words:

" . . . I will answer"

God Said No!

Amy prayed, "Lord please give me blue eyes." Then she climbed into bed, knowing that God would answer her prayer.

God did answer Amy's prayer. He said, "No!"

God had a good reason for saying no. When Amy grew up she became a missionary to India. But she had a problem. The Indian people would not let her into the temple to learn about their worship because she was not Indian. So, she stained her skin with coffee and dressed in Indian clothing. This, plus her dark brown eyes, made her look like an Indian. And she was able to tell many Indian people about Jesus.

Now Amy knew that God's answer was the best answer.

I know God hears and answers prayer,
Though sometimes He answers me
In a way I do not expect Him to,
For He knows what is best, you see!

Hide and Seek Words ☐

As you read your Bible try to find these hidden words:

" . . . Go ye"

Nancee Goes

Nancee had loved music since she was a little girl. When she got older she studied the organ.

Nancee felt God wanted her to be a missionary. She thought, *I want to serve the Lord as a missionary but I will miss my organ and piano. Surely they won't have them out in the jungles where missionaries work.* But Nancee wanted God's will more than anything so she said, "Lord, I'll be a missionary for You!"

God did ask Nancee to be a missionary, but not to the jungle as she had expected! God asked her to be the music director for a missionary ra-dio station. She had her pi-ano and organ and even learned to play the harp!

Are you willing to be a missionary for Jesus? God will guide you to the best place to work for Him.